The gospel according to
St. Matthew

CONTEMPORARY ENGLISH VERSION

CHRIST IN MAJESTY WITH SYMBOLS OF THE EVANGELISTS

The Gospel According to
St. Matthew

Contemporary English Version

American Bible Society
New York

CEV

Imprimatur for New Testament
✠ Most Rev. Daniel E. Pilarczyk
President, National Conference
of Catholic Bishops
March 22, 1991

Design:
Brian Kobberger/Jay Jaffe,
Bill Smith Studio

Photo Credits
front cover:
© Scala/Art Resource, New York, NY
emblem: German 1550 Bible,
Luther vrsn. H. Lufft, Wittenberg, vol. II,
American Bible Society Collection
back cover: © Photodisc, Inc.
frontispiece: The British Library

ISBN 1 – 58516 – 084 – 9

Printed in the United States of America
Eng. Port. CEV560P/Imp. – 107784
ABS – 7/02 – 3,000 – 8,500 — CG3

Welcome to the Contemporary English Version

Languages are spoken before they are written. And far more communication is done through the spoken word than through the written word. In fact, more people *hear* the Bible read than read it for themselves. Traditional translations of the Bible count on the *reader's* ability to understand a *written* text. But the *Contemporary English Version* differs from all other English Bibles—past and present—in that it takes into consideration the needs of the *hearer,* as well as those of the reader, who may not be familiar with traditional biblical language.

The *Contemporary English Version* has been described as a "user-friendly" and a "mission-driven" translation that can be *read aloud* without stumbling, *heard* without misunderstanding, and *listened to* with enjoyment and appreciation, because the language is contemporary and the style is lucid and lyrical.

The *Contemporary English Version* invites you to *read,* to *hear,* to *understand* and to *share*

the Word of God now
as never before!

Introduction to the Gospels

The Gospels provide various pictures of the life and teachings of Jesus Christ. The word "Gospel" comes from an Old English word that means "good news." The Greek word that is translated as "gospel" or "good news" is *euangelion* (see MARK 1.1). The English words "evangelist" and "evangelism" come from this word. An evangelist is one who tells good news.

The Gospels (Matthew, Mark, Luke, and John) were probably written down in their present form between 30 and 60 years after Jesus died and was raised to life by God. Since Jesus himself left no writings, the Gospels record stories and eyewitness descriptions that had been passed on by word of mouth for a number of years. At first, Jesus' followers were so eager to tell the message about him that they didn't think it was necessary to write down what he had said and done. But as Jesus' first followers and eyewitnesses grew older and died, it became more important to have a written record of Jesus and his teachings, and to describe his death and how God brought him back to life.

Although other "gospels" were written, the only ones accepted as reliable by the whole church were MATTHEW, MARK, LUKE, and JOHN. It is not certain who actually wrote the Gospels, since the names of the authors are never given in the books that bear the names of MATTHEW, MARK, LUKE, and JOHN. The Gospels were probably written between A.D. 60, ten years before the temple was destroyed in Jerusalem, and A.D.100. Most scholars agree that MARK was most likely the first Gospel written, since MATTHEW and LUKE seem to take many of their details and the order of events directly from MARK.

Many sources were used to create the Gospels. These probably included various collections of Jesus' sayings and stories that were available to the Gospel writers. For example, a number of Jesus' sayings are similar in MATTHEW and LUKE, so they may have been working with the same source. They also appear to have used MARK for their basic outlines. But MATTHEW and LUKE used different sources to describe the events surrounding Jesus' birth, since MARK begins after Jesus is already grown up. Because MATTHEW, MARK, and LUKE have so much material in common and follow the same basic outline, they are sometimes referred to as the "Synoptic" Gospels (from the Greek word synopsis, which means "seeing together").

These Synoptic Gospels are more like each other than any of them is like the Gospel of JOHN. While MATTHEW, MARK, and LUKE focus on Jesus' public teaching and miracle working in Galilee, JOHN contains information about Jesus' early work in Judea. These include the so-called "I am" sayings, such as "I am the bread that gives life!" (JOHN 6.35); "I am the light for the world!" (John 8.12); and many more. The order of events in JOHN does not follow the order shared by MATTHEW, MARK, and LUKE. And JOHN does not include any of Jesus' stories (parables) that are found in the other three Gospels. Each Gospel presents its own perspective on the events of Jesus' life and his teachings. For more about what makes each of these accounts of Jesus' life and ministry unique, see the Introduction to each Gospel.

Matthew Tells
the Good News

ABOUT THIS BOOK

The Sermon on the Mount (5.1—7.28), the Lord's Prayer (6.9–13), and the Golden Rule (7.12: "Treat others as you want them to treat you") are all in this book. It is perhaps the best known and the most quoted of all the books that have ever been written about Jesus. That is one reason why Matthew was placed first among the four books about Jesus called Gospels.

One of the most important ideas found here is that God expects his people to obey him, and this is what is meant by the Greek word that appears in many translations as *righteousness*. It is used seven times by Matthew, but only once by Luke, and not at all by Mark. So it is an important clue to much of what Matthew wants his readers to understand about the teaching of Jesus.

Jesus first uses this word at his own baptism, when he tells John the Baptist, "We must do all that God wants us to do" (3.15). Then, during his Sermon on the Mount, he speaks five more times of what God's people must do to obey him (5.6,10,20; 6.1,33). And finally, he reminds the chief priests and leaders of the people, "John the Baptist showed you how to do right" (21.32).

Matthew wanted to provide for the people of his time a record of Jesus' message and ministry. It is clear that the Old Testament Scriptures were very important to these people. And Matthew never fails to show when these texts point to the coming of Jesus as the Messiah sent from God. Matthew wrote this book to make sure Christians knew that their faith in Jesus as the Messiah was well anchored in the Old Testament Scriptures, and to help them grow in faith.

Matthew ends his story with the words of Jesus to his followers, which tell what they are to do after he leaves them:

I have been given all authority in heaven and on earth! Go to the people of all nations and make them my disciples. Baptize them in the name of the Father, the Son, and the Holy Spirit, and teach them to do everything I have told you. I will be with you always, even until the end of the world.

(28.18b–20)

A QUICK LOOK AT THIS BOOK

- The Ancestors and Birth of Jesus (1.1—2.23)
- The Message of John the Baptist (3.1–12)
- The Baptism and Temptation of Jesus (3.13—4.11)
- Jesus in Galilee (4.12—18.35)
- Jesus Goes from Galilee to Jerusalem (19.1—20.34)
- Jesus' Last Week: His Trial and Death (21.1—27.66)
- Jesus Is Alive (28.1–20)

The Ancestors of Jesus
(Luke 3.23–38)

1 Jesus Christ came from the family of King David and also from the family of Abraham. And this is a list of his ancestors. 2-6aFrom Abraham to King David, his ancestors were:

Abraham, Isaac, Jacob, Judah and his brothers (Judah's sons were Perez and Zerah, and their mother was Tamar), Hezron;

Ram, Amminadab, Nahshon, Salmon, Boaz (his mother was Rahab), Obed (his mother was Ruth), Jesse, and King David.

6b-11From David to the time of the exile in Babylonia, the ancestors of Jesus were:

David, Solomon (his mother had been Uriah's wife), Rehoboam, Abijah, Asa, Jehoshaphat, Jehoram;

Uzziah, Jotham, Ahaz, Hezekiah, Manasseh, Amon, Josiah, and Jehoiachin and his brothers.

12-16From the exile to the birth of Jesus, his ancestors were:

Jehoiachin, Shealtiel, Zerubbabel, Abiud, Eliakim, Azor, Zadok, Achim;

Eliud, Eleazer, Matthan, Jacob, and Joseph, the husband of Mary, the mother of Jesus, who is called the Messiah.

17There were fourteen generations from Abraham to David. There were also fourteen from David to the exile in Babylonia and fourteen more to the birth of the Messiah.

The Birth of Jesus
(Luke 2.1–7)

18This is how Jesus Christ was born. A young woman named Mary was engaged to Joseph from King David's family. But before they were married, she learned that she was going to have a baby by God's Holy Spirit. 19Joseph was a good man[a] and did not want to embarrass Mary in front of everyone. So he decided to quietly call off the wedding.

20While Joseph was thinking about this, an angel from the Lord came to him in a dream. The angel said, "Joseph, the baby that Mary will have is from the Holy Spirit. Go ahead and marry her. 21Then after her baby is born, name him Jesus,[b] because he will save his people from their sins."

22So God's promise came true, just as the prophet had said, 23"A virgin will have a baby boy, and he will be called Immanuel," which means "God is with us."

24After Joseph woke up, he and Mary were soon married, just as the Lord's angel had told him to do. 25But they did not live together before her baby was born. Then Joseph named him Jesus.

The Wise Men

2 When Jesus was born in the village of Bethlehem in Judea, Herod was king. During this time some wise men[c] from the east came to Jerusalem 2and said, "Where is the child born to be king of the Jews? We saw his star in the east[d] and have come to worship him."

3When King Herod heard about this, he was worried, and so was everyone else in Jerusalem. 4Herod brought together all the chief priests and the

---

[a]good man: Or "kind man," or "man who always did the right thing." [b]name him Jesus: In Hebrew the name "Jesus" means "the Lord saves." [c]wise men: People famous for studying the stars. [d]his star in the east: Or "his star rise."

teachers of the Law of Moses and asked them, "Where will the Messiah be born?"

5They told him, "He will be born in Bethlehem, just as the prophet wrote,

6'Bethlehem in the land
of Judea,
you are very important
among the towns of Judea.
From your town
will come a leader,
who will be like a shepherd
for my people Israel.' "

7Herod secretly called in the wise men and asked them when they had first seen the star. **8**He told them, "Go to Bethlehem and search carefully for the child. As soon as you find him, let me know. I want to go and worship him too."

9The wise men listened to what the king said and then left. And the star they had seen in the east went on ahead of them until it stopped over the place where the child was. **10**They were thrilled and excited to see the star.

11When the men went into the house and saw the child with Mary, his mother, they kneeled down and worshiped him. They took out their gifts of gold, frankincense, and myrrh*e* and gave them to him. **12**Later they were warned in a dream not to return to Herod, and they went back home by another road.

The Escape to Egypt

13After the wise men had gone, an angel from the Lord appeared to Joseph in a dream. The angel said, "Get up! Hurry and take the child and his mother to Egypt! Stay there until I tell you to return, because Herod is looking for the child and wants to kill him."

14That night Joseph got up and took his wife and the child to Egypt, **15**where they stayed until Herod died. So the Lord's promise came true, just as the prophet had said, "I called my son out of Egypt."

The Killing of the Children

16When Herod found out that the wise men from the east had tricked him, he was very angry. He gave orders for his men to kill all the boys who lived in or near Bethlehem and were two years old and younger.

17So the Lord's promise came true, just as the prophet Jeremiah had said,

18"In Ramah a voice was heard
crying and weeping loudly.
Rachel was mourning
for her children,
and she refused
to be comforted,
because they were dead."

The Return from Egypt

19After King Herod died, an angel from the Lord appeared in a dream to Joseph while he was still in Egypt. **20**The angel said, "Get up and take the child and his mother back to Israel. The people who wanted to kill him are now dead."

21Joseph got up and left with them for Israel. **22**But when he heard that Herod's son Archelaus was now ruler of Judea, he was afraid to go there. Then in a dream he was told to go to Galilee, **23**and they went to live there

---

efrankincense, and myrrh: Frankincense was a valuable powder that was burned to make a sweet smell. Myrrh was a valuable sweet-smelling powder often used in perfume.

in the town of Nazareth. So the Lord's promise came true, just as the prophet had said, "He will be called a Nazarene."*f*

The Preaching of John the Baptist
(Mark 1.1–8; Luke 3.1–18; John 1.19–28)

3 Years later John the Baptist started preaching in the desert of Judea. 2He said, "Turn back to God! The kingdom of heaven*g* will soon be here."*h*

3John was the one the prophet Isaiah was talking about, when he said,

"In the desert someone
    is shouting,
'Get the road ready
    for the Lord!
Make a straight path
    for him.' "

4John wore clothes made of camel's hair. He had a leather strap around his waist and ate grasshoppers and wild honey.

5From Jerusalem and all Judea and from the Jordan River Valley crowds of people went to John. 6They told how sorry they were for their sins, and he baptized them in the river.

7Many Pharisees and Sadducees also came to be baptized. But John said to them:

You bunch of snakes! Who warned you to run from the coming judgment? 8Do something to show that you have really given up your sins. 9And don't start telling yourselves that you belong to Abraham's family. I tell you that God can turn these stones into children for Abraham. 10An ax is ready to cut the trees down at their roots. Any tree that does not produce good fruit will be chopped down and thrown into a fire.

11I baptize you with water so that you will give up your sins.*i* But someone more powerful is going to come, and I am not good enough even to carry his sandals.*j* He will baptize you with the Holy Spirit and with fire. 12His threshing fork is in his hand, and he is ready to separate the wheat from the husks.*k* He will store the wheat in a barn and burn the husks in a fire that never goes out.

The Baptism of Jesus
(Mark 1.9–11; Luke 3.21, 22)

13Jesus left Galilee and went to the Jordan River to be baptized by John. 14But John kept objecting and said, "I ought to be baptized by you. Why have you come to me?"

15Jesus answered, "For now this is how it should be, because we must do all that God wants us to do." Then John agreed.

16So Jesus was baptized. And as soon as he came out of the water, the sky opened, and he saw the Spirit of

---

f He will be called a Nazarene: The prophet who said this is not known. *g kingdom of heaven*: In the Gospel of Matthew "kingdom of heaven" is used with the same meaning as "God's kingdom" in Mark and Luke. *h will soon be here*: Or "is already here." *i so that you will give up your sins*: Or "because you have given up your sins." *j carry his sandals*: This was one of the duties of a slave. *k His threshing fork is in his hand, and he is ready to separate the wheat from the husks*: After Jewish farmers had trampled out the grain, they used a large fork to pitch the grain and the husks into the air. Wind would blow away the light husks, and the grain would fall back to the ground, where it could be gathered up.

God coming down on him like a dove. 17Then a voice from heaven said, "This is my own dear Son, and I am pleased with him."

Jesus and the Devil
(Mark 1.12, 13; Luke 4.1–13)

4 The Holy Spirit led Jesus into the desert, so that the devil could test him. 2After Jesus went without eating*l* for forty days and nights, he was very hungry. 3Then the devil came to him and said, "If you are God's Son, tell these stones to turn into bread."

4Jesus answered, "The Scriptures say:

'No one can live only on food.
People need every word
that God has spoken.' "

5Next, the devil took Jesus to the holy city and had him stand on the highest part of the temple. 6The devil said, "If you are God's Son, jump off. The Scriptures say:

'God will give his angels
orders about you.
They will catch you
in their arms,
and you will not hurt
your feet on the stones.' "

7Jesus answered, "The Scriptures also say, 'Don't try to test the Lord your God!' "

8Finally, the devil took Jesus up on a very high mountain and showed him all the kingdoms on earth and their power. 9The devil said to him, "I will give all this to you, if you will bow down and worship me."

10Jesus answered, "Go away Satan! The Scriptures say:

'Worship the Lord your God
and serve only him.' "

11Then the devil left Jesus, and angels came to help him.

Jesus Begins His Work
(Mark 1.14, 15; Luke 4.14, 15)

12When Jesus heard that John had been put in prison, he went to Galilee. 13But instead of staying in Nazareth, Jesus moved to Capernaum. This town was beside Lake Galilee in the territory of Zebulun and Naphtali.*m* 14So God's promise came true, just as the prophet Isaiah had said,

15"Listen, lands of Zebulun
and Naphtali,
lands along the road
to the sea and west
of the Jordan!
Listen Galilee,
land of the Gentiles!
16Although your people
live in darkness,
they will see
a bright light.
Although they live
in the shadow of death,
a light will shine
on them."

17Then Jesus started preaching, "Turn back to God! The kingdom of heaven will soon be here."*n*

Jesus Chooses Four Fishermen
(Mark 1.16–20; Luke 5.1–11)

18While Jesus was walking along the shore of Lake Galilee, he saw two

---

*l*went without eating: The Jewish people sometimes went without eating (also called "fasting") to show their love for God and to become better followers.   *m*Zebulun and Naphtali: In Old Testament times these tribes were in northern Palestine, and in New Testament times many Gentiles lived where these tribes had once been.   *n*The kingdom of heaven will soon be here: See the two notes at 3.2.

brothers. One was Simon, also known as Peter, and the other was Andrew. They were fishermen, and they were casting their net into the lake. 19Jesus said to them, "Come with me! I will teach you how to bring in people instead of fish." 20Right then the two brothers dropped their nets and went with him.

21Jesus walked on until he saw James and John, the sons of Zebedee. They were in a boat with their father, mending their nets. Jesus asked them to come with him too. 22Right away they left the boat and their father and went with Jesus.

Jesus Teaches, Preaches, and Heals
(Luke 6.17–19)

23Jesus went all over Galilee, teaching in the Jewish meeting places and preaching the good news about God's kingdom. He also healed every kind of disease and sickness. 24News about him spread all over Syria, and people with every kind of sickness or disease were brought to him. Some of them had a lot of demons in them, others were thought to be crazy,*o* and still others could not walk. But Jesus healed them all.

25Large crowds followed Jesus from Galilee and the region around the ten cities known as Decapolis.*p* They also came from Jerusalem, Judea, and from across the Jordan River.

The Sermon on the Mount

5 When Jesus saw the crowds, he went up on the side of a mountain and sat down.*q*

Blessings
(Luke 6.20–23)

Jesus' disciples gathered around him, 2and he taught them:
> 3God blesses those people
>   who depend only on him.
> They belong to the kingdom
>   of heaven!*r*
> 4God blesses those people
>   who grieve.
> They will find comfort!
> 5God blesses those people
>   who are humble.
> The earth will belong
>   to them!
> 6God blesses those people
>   who want to obey him*s*
>   more than to eat or drink.
> They will be given
>   what they want!
> 7God blesses those people
>   who are merciful.
> They will be treated
>   with mercy!
> 8God blesses those people
>   whose hearts are pure.
> They will see him!
> 9God blesses those people
>   who make peace.
> They will be called
>   his children!

---

othought to be crazy: In ancient times people with epilepsy were thought to be crazy. *pthe ten cities known as Decapolis*: A group of ten cities east of Samaria and Galilee, where the people followed the Greek way of life. *qsat down*: Teachers in the ancient world, including Jewish teachers, usually sat down when they taught. *rThey belong to the kingdom of heaven*: Or "The kingdom of heaven belongs to them." *swho want to obey him*: Or "who want to do right" or "who want everyone to be treated right."

10God blesses those people
who are treated badly
for doing right.
They belong to the kingdom
of heaven.*

11God will bless you when people insult you, mistreat you, and tell all kinds of evil lies about you because of me. 12Be happy and excited! You will have a great reward in heaven. People did these same things to the prophets who lived long ago.

Salt and Light
(Mark 9.50; Luke 14.34, 35)

13You are like salt for everyone on earth. But if salt no longer tastes like salt, how can it make food salty? All it is good for is to be thrown out and walked on. 14You are like light for the whole world. A city built on top of a hill cannot be hidden, 15and no one would light a lamp and put it under a clay pot. A lamp is placed on a lamp stand, where it can give light to everyone in the house. 16Make your light shine, so that others will see the good that you do and will praise your Father in heaven.

The Law of Moses

17Don't suppose that I came to do away with the Law and the Prophets.* I did not come to do away with them, but to give them their full meaning. 18Heaven and earth may disappear. But I promise you that not even a period or comma will ever disappear from the Law. Everything written in it must happen.

19If you reject even the least important command in the Law and teach others to do the same, you will be the least important person in the kingdom of heaven. But if you obey and teach others its commands, you will have an important place in the kingdom. 20You must obey God's commands better than the Pharisees and the teachers of the Law obey them. If you don't, I promise you that you will never get into the kingdom of heaven.

Anger

21You know that our ancestors were told, "Do not murder" and "A murderer must be brought to trial." 22But I promise you that if you are angry with someone,* you will have to stand trial. If you call someone a fool, you will be taken to court. And if you say that someone is worthless, you will be in danger of the fires of hell.

23So if you are about to place your gift on the altar and remember that someone is angry with you, 24leave your gift there in front of the altar. Make peace with that person, then come back and offer your gift to God.

25Before you are dragged into court, make friends with the person who has accused you of doing wrong. If you don't, you will be

---

They belong to the kingdom of heaven: See the note at 5.3.   *the Law and the Prophets*: The Jewish Scriptures, that is, the Old Testament.   *someone*: In verses 22-24 the Greek text has "brother," which may refer to people in general or to other followers.

handed over to the judge and then to the officer who will put you in jail. 26I promise you that you will not get out until you have paid the last cent you owe.

Marriage

27You know the commandment which says, "Be faithful in marriage." 28But I tell you that if you look at another woman and want her, you are already unfaithful in your thoughts. 29If your right eye causes you to sin, poke it out and throw it away. It is better to lose one part of your body, than for your whole body to end up in hell. 30If your right hand causes you to sin, chop it off and throw it away! It is better to lose one part of your body, than for your whole body to be thrown into hell.

Divorce
(Matthew 19.9; Mark 10.11, 12; Luke 16.18)

31You have been taught that a man who divorces his wife must write out divorce papers for her.*w* 32But I tell you not to divorce your wife unless she has committed some terrible sexual sin.*x* If you divorce her, you will cause her to be unfaithful, just as any man who marries her is guilty of taking another man's wife.

Promises

33You know that our ancestors were told, "Don't use the Lord's name to make a promise unless you are going to keep it." 34But I tell you not to swear by anything when you make a promise! Heaven is God's throne, so don't swear by heaven. 35The earth is God's footstool, so don't swear by the earth. Jerusalem is the city of the great king, so don't swear by it. 36Don't swear by your own head. You cannot make one hair white or black. 37When you make a promise, say only "Yes" or "No." Anything else comes from the devil.

Revenge
(Luke 6.29, 30)

38You know that you have been taught, "An eye for an eye and a tooth for a tooth." 39But I tell you not to try to get even with a person who has done something to you. When someone slaps your right cheek,*y* turn and let that person slap your other cheek. 40If someone sues you for your shirt, give up your coat as well. 41If a soldier forces you to carry his pack one mile, carry it two miles.*z* 42When people ask you for something, give it to them. When they want to borrow money, loan it to them.

---

w write out divorce papers for her: Jewish men could divorce their wives, but the women could not divorce their husbands. The purpose of writing these papers was to make it harder for a man to divorce his wife. Before this law was made, all a man had to do was to send his wife away and say that she was no longer his wife.   *x some terrible sexual sin*: This probably refers to the laws about the wrong kinds of marriages that are forbidden in Leviticus or to some serious sexual sin.   *y right cheek*: A slap on the right cheek was a bad insult.   *z two miles*: A Roman soldier had the right to force a person to carry his pack as far as one mile.

Love
(Luke 6.27, 28, 32–36)

43You have heard people say, "Love your neighbors and hate your enemies." **44**But I tell you to love your enemies and pray for anyone who mistreats you. **45**Then you will be acting like your Father in heaven. He makes the sun rise on both good and bad people. And he sends rain for the ones who do right and for the ones who do wrong. **46**If you love only those people who love you, will God reward you for that? Even tax collectors*a* love their friends. **47**If you greet only your friends, what's so great about that? Don't even unbelievers do that? **48**But you must always act like your Father in heaven.

Giving

6 When you do good deeds, don't try to show off. If you do, you won't get a reward from your Father in heaven.

2When you give to the poor, don't blow a loud horn. That's what showoffs do in the meeting places and on the street corners, because they are always looking for praise. I promise you that they already have their reward.

3When you give to the poor, don't let anyone know about it.*b* **4**Then your gift will be given in secret. Your Father knows what is done in secret, and he will reward you.

Prayer
(Luke 11.2–4)

5When you pray, don't be like those showoffs who love to stand up and pray in the meeting places and on the street corners. They do this just to look good. I promise you that they already have their reward.

6When you pray, go into a room alone and close the door. Pray to your Father in private. He knows what is done in private, and he will reward you.

7When you pray, don't talk on and on as people do who don't know God. They think God likes to hear long prayers. **8**Don't be like them. Your Father knows what you need before you ask.

9You should pray like this:
Our Father in heaven,
  help us to honor
    your name.
10Come and set up
    your kingdom,
  so that everyone on earth
    will obey you,
  as you are obeyed
    in heaven.
11Give us our food for today.*c*
12Forgive our sins,
    as we forgive others.*d*

---

*a*tax collectors: These were usually Jewish people who paid the Romans for the right to collect taxes. They were hated by other Jews who thought of them as traitors to their country and to their religion. *b*don't let anyone know about it: The Greek text has, "Don't let your left hand know what your right hand is doing." *c*our food for today: Or "the food that we need" or "our food for the coming day." *d*sins . . . others: Or "what we owe . . . what others owe."

13Keep us from being tempted and protect us from evil.*e*

14If you forgive others for the wrongs they do to you, your Father in heaven will forgive you. 15But if you don't forgive others, your Father will not forgive your sins.

Worshiping God by Going without Eating

16When you go without eating,*f* don't try to look gloomy as those showoffs do when they go without eating. I promise you that they already have their reward. 17Instead, comb your hair and wash your face. 18Then others won't know that you are going without eating. But your Father sees what is done in private, and he will reward you.

Treasures in Heaven
(Luke 12.33, 34)

19Don't store up treasures on earth! Moths and rust can destroy them, and thieves can break in and steal them. 20Instead, store up your treasures in heaven, where moths and rust cannot destroy them, and thieves cannot break in and steal them. 21Your heart will always be where your treasure is.

Light
(Luke 11.34–36)

22Your eyes are like a window for your body. When they are good, you have all the light you need. 23But when your eyes are bad, everything is dark. If the light inside you is dark, you surely are in the dark.

Money
(Luke 16.13)

24You cannot be the slave of two masters! You will like one more than the other or be more loyal to one than the other. You cannot serve both God and money.

Worry
(Luke 12.22–31)

25I tell you not to worry about your life. Don't worry about having something to eat, drink, or wear. Isn't life more than food or clothing? 26Look at the birds in the sky! They don't plant or harvest. They don't even store grain in barns. Yet your Father in heaven takes care of them. Aren't you worth more than birds?

27Can worry make you live longer?*g* 28Why worry about clothes? Look how the wild flowers grow. They don't work hard to make their clothes. 29But I tell you that Solomon with all his wealth*h* was not as well clothed as one of them. 30God gives such beauty to everything that grows in the fields, even though it is here today and thrown into a fire tomorrow. He will surely do even

---

eevil: Or "the evil one," that is, the devil. Some manuscripts add, "The kingdom, the power, and the glory are yours forever. Amen." *fwithout eating*: See the note at 4.2. *glive longer*: Or "grow taller." *hSolomon with all his wealth*: The Jewish people thought that Solomon was the richest person who had ever lived.

more for you! Why do you have such little faith?

31Don't worry and ask yourselves, "Will we have anything to eat? Will we have anything to drink? Will we have any clothes to wear?" **32**Only people who don't know God are always worrying about such things. Your Father in heaven knows that you need all of these. **33**But more than anything else, put God's work first and do what he wants. Then all the other things will be yours as well.

34Don't worry about tomorrow. It will take care of itself. You have enough to worry about today.

Judging Others
(Luke 6.37, 38, 41, 42)

7 Don't condemn others, and God will not condemn you. **2**God will be as hard on you as you are on others! He will treat you exactly as you treat them.

3You can see the speck in your friend's eye, but you don't notice the log in your own eye. **4**How can you say, "My friend, let me take the speck out of your eye," when you don't see the log in your own eye? **5**You're nothing but showoffs! First, take the log out of your own eye. Then you can see how to take the speck out of your friend's eye.

6Don't give to dogs what belongs to God. They will only turn and attack you. Don't throw pearls down in front of pigs. They will trample all over them.

Ask, Search, Knock
(Luke 11.9–13)

7Ask, and you will receive. Search, and you will find. Knock, and the door will be opened for you. **8**Everyone who asks will receive. Everyone who searches will find. And the door will be opened for everyone who knocks. **9**Would any of you give your hungry child a stone, if the child asked for some bread? **10**Would you give your child a snake if the child asked for a fish? **11**As bad as you are, you still know how to give good gifts to your children. But your heavenly Father is even more ready to give good things to people who ask.

12Treat others as you want them to treat you. This is what the Law and the Prophets*ᶦ* are all about.

The Narrow Gate
(Luke 13.24)

13Go in through the narrow gate. The gate to destruction is wide, and the road that leads there is easy to follow. A lot of people go through that gate. **14**But the gate to life is very narrow. The road that leads there is so hard to follow that only a few people find it.

A Tree and Its Fruit
(Luke 6.43–45)

15Watch out for false prophets! They dress up like sheep, but inside they are wolves who have

---

ᶦthe Law and the Prophets: See the note at 5.17.

come to attack you. [16]You can tell what they are by what they do. No one picks grapes or figs from thorn bushes. [17]A good tree produces good fruit, and a bad tree produces bad fruit. [18]A good tree cannot produce bad fruit, and a bad tree cannot produce good fruit. [19]Every tree that produces bad fruit will be chopped down and burned. [20]You can tell who the false prophets are by their deeds.

A Warning
(Luke 13.26, 27)

[21]Not everyone who calls me their Lord will get into the kingdom of heaven. Only the ones who obey my Father in heaven will get in. [22]On the day of judgment many will call me their Lord. They will say, "We preached in your name, and in your name we forced out demons and worked many miracles." [23]But I will tell them, "I will have nothing to do with you! Get out of my sight, you evil people!"

Two Builders
(Luke 6.47–49)

[24]Anyone who hears and obeys these teachings of mine is like a wise person who built a house on solid rock. [25]Rain poured down, rivers flooded, and winds beat against that house. But it did not fall, because it was built on solid rock.

[26]Anyone who hears my teachings and does not obey them is like a foolish person who built a house on sand. [27]The rain poured down, the rivers flooded, and the winds blew and beat against that house. Finally, it fell with a crash.

[28]When Jesus finished speaking, the crowds were surprised at his teaching. [29]He taught them like someone with authority, and not like their teachers of the Law of Moses.

Jesus Heals a Man
(Mark 1.40–45; Luke 5.12–16)

8 As Jesus came down the mountain, he was followed by large crowds. [2]Suddenly a man with leprosy[j] came and kneeled in front of Jesus. He said, "Lord, you have the power to make me well, if only you wanted to."

[3]Jesus put his hand on the man and said, "I do want to! Now you are well." At once the man's leprosy disappeared. [4]Jesus told him, "Don't tell anyone about this, but go and show the priest that you are well. Then take a gift to the temple just as Moses commanded, and everyone will know that you have been healed."[k]

Jesus Heals an Army Officer's Servant
(Luke 7.1–10; John 4.43–54)

[5]When Jesus was going into the town of Capernaum, an army officer

---

[j]*leprosy*: In biblical times the word "leprosy" was used for many different kinds of skin diseases.
[k]*everyone will know that you have been healed*: People with leprosy had to be examined by a priest and told that they were well (that is "clean") before they could once again live a normal life in the Jewish community. The gift that Moses commanded was the sacrifice of some lambs together with flour mixed with olive oil.

came up to him and said, 6"Lord, my servant is at home in such terrible pain that he can't even move."

7"I will go and heal him," Jesus replied.

8But the officer said, "Lord, I'm not good enough for you to come into my house. Just give the order, and my servant will get well. 9I have officers who give orders to me, and I have soldiers who take orders from me. I can say to one of them, 'Go!' and he goes. I can say to another, 'Come!' and he comes. I can say to my servant, 'Do this!' and he will do it."

10When Jesus heard this, he was so surprised that he turned and said to the crowd following him, "I tell you that in all of Israel I've never found anyone with this much faith! 11Many people will come from everywhere to enjoy the feast in the kingdom of heaven with Abraham, Isaac, and Jacob. 12But the ones who should have been in the kingdom will be thrown out into the dark. They will cry and grit their teeth in pain."

13Then Jesus said to the officer, "You may go home now. Your faith has made it happen."

Right then his servant was healed.

Jesus Heals Many People
(Mark 1.29–34; Luke 4.38–41)

14Jesus went to the home of Peter, where he found that Peter's mother-in-law was sick in bed with fever. 15He took her by the hand, and the fever left her. Then she got up and served Jesus a meal.

16That evening many people with demons in them were brought to Jesus. And with only a word he forced out the evil spirits and healed everyone who was sick. 17So God's promise came true, just as the prophet Isaiah had said,

"He healed our diseases
and made us well."

Some Who Wanted to Go with Jesus
(Luke 9.57–62)

18When Jesus saw the crowd,*l* he went across Lake Galilee. 19A teacher of the Law of Moses came up to him and said, "Teacher, I'll go anywhere with you!"

20Jesus replied, "Foxes have dens, and birds have nests. But the Son of Man does not have a place to call his own."

21Another disciple said to Jesus, "Lord, let me wait till I bury my father."

22Jesus answered, "Come with me, and let the dead bury their dead." *m*

A Storm
(Mark 4.35–41; Luke 8.22–25)

23After Jesus left in a boat with his disciples, 24a terrible storm suddenly struck the lake, and waves started splashing into their boat.

Jesus was sound asleep, 25so the disciples went over to him and woke him up. They said, "Lord, save us! We're going to drown!"

26But Jesus replied, "Why are you so afraid? You surely don't have much faith." Then he got up and ordered the

---

l saw the crowd: Some manuscripts have "large crowd." Others have "large crowds." *m let the dead bury their dead*: For the Jewish people a proper burial of their dead was a very important duty. But Jesus teaches that following him is even more important.

wind and the waves to calm down. And
everything was calm.
27 The men in the boat were
amazed and said, "Who is this? Even
the wind and the waves obey him."

Two Men with Demons in Them
(Mark 5.1–20; Luke 8.26–39)

28 After Jesus had crossed the lake,
he came to shore near the town of Gadara[n] and started down the road. Two
men with demons in them came to him
from the tombs.[o] They were so fierce
that no one could travel that way.
29 Suddenly they shouted, "Jesus, Son
of God, what do you want with us?
Have you come to punish us before our
time?"
30 Not far from there a large herd
of pigs was feeding. 31 So the demons
begged Jesus, "If you force us out,
please send us into those pigs!" 32 Jesus
told them to go, and they went out of
the men and into the pigs. All at once
the pigs rushed down the steep bank
into the lake and drowned.
33 The people taking care of the
pigs ran to the town and told everything, especially what had happened
to the two men. 34 Everyone in town
came out to meet Jesus. When they
saw him, they begged him to leave
their part of the country.

Jesus Heals a Crippled Man
(Mark 2.1–12; Luke 5.17–26)

9 Jesus got into a boat and crossed
back over to the town where he
lived.[p] 2 Some people soon brought to
him a crippled man lying on a mat.
When Jesus saw how much faith the
had, he said to the crippled man, "M
friend, don't worry! Your sins are for
given."
3 Some teachers of the Law of Mo
ses said to themselves, "Jesus mus
think he is God!"
4 But Jesus knew what was in thei
minds, and he said, "Why are you
thinking such evil things? 5 Is it easie
for me to tell this crippled man tha
his sins are forgiven or to tell him t
get up and walk? 6 But I will show you
that the Son of Man has the right t
forgive sins here on earth." So Jesus
said to the man, "Get up! Pick up you
mat and go on home." 7 The man go
up and went home. 8 When the crowd
saw this, they were afraid[q] and praise
God for giving such authority to people

Jesus Chooses Matthew
(Mark 2.13–17; Luke 5.27–32)

9 As Jesus was leaving, he saw a
tax collector[r] named Matthew sitting
at the place for paying taxes. Jesus said
to him, "Come with me." Matthew got
up and went with him.
10 Later, Jesus and his disciples
were having dinner at Matthew's
house.[s] Many tax collectors and other
sinners were also there. 11 Some Pharisees asked Jesus' disciples, "Why does
your teacher eat with tax collectors and
other sinners?"
12 Jesus heard them and answered,
"Healthy people don't need a doctor,
but sick people do. 13 Go and learn what
the Scriptures mean when they say,
'Instead of offering sacrifices to me, I

[n] *Gadara*: Some manuscripts have "Gergasa." Others have "Gerasa." [o] *tombs*: It was thought that demons and evil spirits lived in tombs and in caves that were used for burying the dead. [p] *where he lived*: Capernaum. See 4.13. [q] *afraid*: Some manuscripts have "amazed." [r] *tax collector*: See the note at 5.46. [s] *Matthew's house*: Or "Jesus' house."

vant you to be merciful to others.' I didn't come to invite good people to be my followers. I came to invite sinners."

People Ask about Going without Eating
(Mark 2.18–22; Luke 5.33–39)

14One day some followers of John the Baptist came and asked Jesus, Why do we and the Pharisees often go without eating,*t* while your disciples never do?"

15Jesus answered:

The friends of a bridegroom don't go without eating while he is still with them. But the time will come when he will be taken from them. Then they will go without eating.

16No one uses a new piece of cloth to patch old clothes. The patch would shrink and tear a bigger hole.

17No one pours new wine into old wineskins. The wine would swell and burst the old skins.*u* Then the wine would be lost, and the skins would be ruined. New wine must be put into new wineskins. Both the skins and the wine will then be safe.

A Dead Girl and a Sick Woman
(Mark 5.21–43; Luke 8.40–56)

18While Jesus was still speaking, a Jewish official came and kneeled in front of him. The man said, "My daughter has just now died! Please come and place your hand on her. Then she will live again."

19Jesus and his disciples got up and went with the man.

20A woman who had been bleeding for twelve years came up behind Jesus and barely touched his clothes. 21She had said to herself, "If I can just touch his clothes, I will get well."

22Jesus turned. He saw the woman and said, "Don't worry! You are now well because of your faith." At that moment she was healed.

23When Jesus went into the home of the Jewish official and saw the musicians and the crowd of mourners,*v* 24he said, "Get out of here! The little girl is not dead. She is just asleep." Everyone started laughing at Jesus. 25But after the crowd had been sent out of the house, Jesus went to the girl's bedside. He took her by the hand and helped her up.

26News about this spread all over that part of the country.

Jesus Heals Two Blind Men

27As Jesus was walking along, two blind men began following him and shouting, "Son of David,*w* have pity on us!"

28After Jesus had gone indoors, the two blind men came up to him. He asked them, "Do you believe I can make you well?"

"Yes, Lord," they answered.

---

t without eating: See the note at 4.2.   *u swell and burst the old skins*: While the juice from grapes was becoming wine, it would swell and stretch the skins in which it had been stored. If the skins were old and stiff, they would burst.   *v the crowd of mourners*: The Jewish people often hired mourners for funerals.   *w Son of David*: The Jewish people expected the Messiah to be from the family of King David, and for this reason the Messiah was often called the "Son of David."

29Jesus touched their eyes and said, "Because of your faith, you will be healed." 30They were able to see, and Jesus strictly warned them not to tell anyone about him. 31But they left and talked about him to everyone in that part of the country.

Jesus Heals a Man Who Could Not Talk

32As Jesus and his disciples were on their way, some people brought to him a man who could not talk because a demon was in him. 33After Jesus had forced the demon out, the man started talking. The crowds were so amazed that they began saying, "Nothing like this has ever happened in Israel!"

34But the Pharisees said, "The leader of the demons gives him the power to force out demons."

Jesus Has Pity on People

35Jesus went to every town and village. He taught in their meeting places and preached the good news about God's kingdom. Jesus also healed every kind of disease and sickness. 36When he saw the crowds, he felt sorry for them. They were confused and helpless, like sheep without a shepherd. 37He said to his disciples, "A large crop is in the fields, but there are only a few workers. 38Ask the Lord in charge of the harvest to send out workers to bring it in."

Jesus Chooses His Twelve Apostles
(Mark 3.13–19; Luke 6.12–16)

10 Jesus called together his twelve disciples. He gave them the power to force out evil spirits and to heal every kind of disease and sickness. 2The first of the twelve apostles was Simon, better known as Peter. His brother Andrew was an apostle, and so were James and John, the two sons of Zebedee. 3Philip, Bartholomew, Thomas, Matthew the tax collector,*x* James the son of Alphaeus, and Thaddaeus were also apostles. 4The others were Simon, known as the Eager One,*y* and Judas Iscariot,*z* who later betrayed Jesus.

Instructions for the Twelve Apostles
(Mark 6.7–13; Luke 9.1–6)

5Jesus sent out the twelve apostles with these instructions:

Stay away from the Gentiles and don't go to any Samaritan town. 6Go only to the people of Israel, because they are like a flock of lost sheep. 7As you go, announce that the kingdom of heaven will soon be here.*a* 8Heal the sick, raise the dead to life, heal people who have leprosy,*b* and force out demons. You received without paying, now give without being paid. 9Don't take along any gold, silver, or copper coins. 10And don't carry*c* a travel-

---

*x*tax collector: See the note at 5.46.   *y*known as the Eager One: The Greek text has "Cananaean," which probably comes from a Hebrew word meaning "zealous" (see Luke 6.15). "Zealot" was the name later given to the members of a Jewish group which resisted and fought against the Romans.   *z*Iscariot: This may mean "a man from Kerioth" (a place in Judea). But more probably it means "a man who was a liar" or "a man who was a betrayer." *a*will soon be here: Or "is already here."   *b*leprosy: See the note at 8.2.   *c*Don't take along . . . don't carry: Or "Don't accept . . . don't accept."

ing bag or an extra shirt or sandals or a walking stick.

Workers deserve their food. 11So when you go to a town or a village, find someone worthy enough to have you as their guest and stay with them until you leave. 12When you go to a home, give it your blessing of peace. 13If the home is deserving, let your blessing remain with them. But if the home is not deserving, take back your blessing of peace. 14If someone won't welcome you or listen to your message, leave their home or town. And shake the dust from your feet at them.*d* 15I promise you that the day of judgment will be easier for the towns of Sodom and Gomorrah*e* than for that town.

Warning about Trouble
(Mark 13.9–13; Luke 21.12–17)

16I am sending you like lambs into a pack of wolves. So be as wise as snakes and as innocent as doves. 17Watch out for people who will take you to court and have you beaten in their meeting places. 18Because of me, you will be dragged before rulers and kings to tell them and the Gentiles about your faith. 19But when someone arrests you, don't worry about what you will say or how you will say it. At that time you will be given the words to say. 20But you will not really be the one speaking. The Spirit from your Father will tell you what to say.

21Brothers and sisters will betray one another and have each other put to death. Parents will betray their own children, and children will turn against their parents and have them killed. 22Everyone will hate you because of me. But if you remain faithful until the end, you will be saved. 23When people mistreat you in one town, hurry to another one. I promise you that before you have gone to all the towns of Israel, the Son of Man will come.

24Disciples are not better than their teacher, and slaves are not better than their master. 25It is enough for disciples to be like their teacher and for slaves to be like their master. If people call the head of the family Satan, what will they say about the rest of the family?

The One to Fear
(Luke 12.2–7)

26Don't be afraid of anyone! Everything that is hidden will be found out, and every secret will be known. 27Whatever I say to you in the dark, you must tell in the light. And you must announce from the housetops whatever I have whispered to you. 28Don't be afraid of people. They can kill you, but they cannot harm your soul. Instead, you should fear God who can destroy both your body and your soul in hell. 29Aren't two sparrows sold

---

*d*shake the dust from your feet at them: This was a way of showing rejection. See Acts 13.51.
*e*Sodom and Gomorrah: During the time of Abraham the Lord destroyed these towns because the people there were so evil.

for only a penny? But your Father knows when any one of them falls to the ground. 30Even the hairs on your head are counted. 31So don't be afraid! You are worth much more than many sparrows.

Telling Others about Christ
(Luke 12.8, 9)

32If you tell others that you belong to me, I will tell my Father in heaven that you are my followers. 33But if you reject me, I will tell my Father in heaven that you don't belong to me.

Not Peace, but Trouble
(Luke 12.51–53; 14.26, 27)

34Don't think that I came to bring peace to the earth! I came to bring trouble, not peace. 35I came to turn sons against their fathers, daughters against their mothers, and daughters-in-law against their mothers-in-law. 36Your worst enemies will be in your own family.

37If you love your father or mother or even your sons and daughters more than me, you are not fit to be my disciples. 38And unless you are willing to take up your cross and come with me, you are not fit to be my disciples. 39If you try to save your life, you will lose it. But if you give it up for me, you will surely find it.

Rewards
(Mark 9.41)

40Anyone who welcomes you welcomes me. And anyone who welcomes me also welcomes the one who sent me. 41Anyone who welcomes a prophet, just because that person is a prophet, will be given the same reward as a prophet. Anyone who welcomes a good person, just because that person is good, will be given the same reward as a good person. 42And anyone who gives one of my most humble followers a cup of cool water, just because that person is my follower, will surely be rewarded.

John the Baptist
(Luke 7.18–35)

11 After Jesus had finished instructing his twelve disciples he left and began teaching and preaching in the towns.*f*

2John was in prison when he heard what Christ was doing. So John sent some of his followers 3to ask Jesus "Are you the one we should be looking for? Or must we wait for someone else?"

4Jesus answered, "Go and tell John what you have heard and seen. 5The blind are now able to see, and the lame can walk. People with leprosy*g* are being healed, and the deaf can hear. The dead are raised to life, and the poor are hearing the good news. 6God will bless everyone who does not reject me because of what I do."

7As John's followers were going away, Jesus spoke to the crowds about John:

What sort of person did you go out into the desert to see? Was

---

fthe towns: The Greek text has "their towns," which may refer to the towns of Galilee or to the towns where Jesus' disciples had lived.   *gleprosy*: See the note at 8.2.

he like tall grass blown about by the wind? 8What kind of man did you go out to see? Was he someone dressed in fine clothes? People who dress like that live in the king's palace. 9What did you really go out to see? Was he a prophet? He certainly was. I tell you that he was more than a prophet. 10In the Scriptures God says about him, "I am sending my messenger ahead of you to get things ready for you." 11I tell you that no one ever born on this earth is greater than John the Baptist. But whoever is least in the kingdom of heaven is greater than John.

12From the time of John the Baptist until now, violent people have been trying to take over the kingdom of heaven by force. 13All the Books of the Prophets and the Law of Moses*h* told what was going to happen up to the time of John. 14And if you believe them, John is Elijah, the prophet you are waiting for. 15If you have ears, pay attention!

16You people are like children sitting in the market and 17shouting to each other,

"We played the flute,
    but you would not dance!
We sang a funeral song,
    but you would not mourn!"

18John the Baptist did not go around eating and drinking, and you said, "That man has a demon in him!" 19But the Son of Man goes around eating and drinking, and you say, "That man eats and drinks too much! He is even a friend of tax collectors*i* and sinners." Yet Wisdom is shown to be right by what it does.

The Unbelieving Towns
(Luke 10.13–15)

20In the towns where Jesus had worked most of his miracles, the people refused to turn to God. So Jesus was upset with them and said:

21You people of Chorazin are in for trouble! You people of Bethsaida are in for trouble too! If the miracles that took place in your towns had happened in Tyre and Sidon, the people there would have turned to God long ago. They would have dressed in sackcloth and put ashes on their heads.*j* 22I tell you that on the day of judgment the people of Tyre and Sidon will get off easier than you will.

23People of Capernaum, do you think you will be honored in heaven? You will go down to hell! If the miracles that took place in your town had happened in Sodom, that town would still be standing. 24So I tell you that on the day of judgment the people of Sodom will get off easier than you.

Come to Me and Rest
(Luke 10.21, 22)

25At that moment Jesus said:
My Father, Lord of heaven and earth, I am grateful that you hid

---

h the Books of the Prophets and the Law of Moses: The Jewish Scriptures, that is, the Old Testament. *i tax collectors*: See the note at 5.46. *j sackcloth . . . ashes on their heads*: This was one way that people showed how sorry they were for their sins.

all this from wise and educated people and showed it to ordinary people. 26Yes, Father, that is what pleased you.

27My Father has given me everything, and he is the only one who knows the Son. The only one who truly knows the Father is the Son. But the Son wants to tell others about the Father, so that they can know him too.

28If you are tired from carrying heavy burdens, come to me and I will give you rest. 29Take the yoke^k I give you. Put it on your shoulders and learn from me. I am gentle and humble, and you will find rest. 30This yoke is easy to bear, and this burden is light.

A Question about the Sabbath
(Mark 2.23–28; Luke 6.1–5)

12 One Sabbath Jesus and his disciples were walking through some wheat fields.^{l} His disciples were hungry and began picking and eating grains of wheat. 2Some Pharisees said to Jesus, "Why are your disciples picking grain on the Sabbath? They are not supposed to do that!"

3Jesus answered:

You surely must have read what David did when he and his followers were hungry. 4He went into the house of God, and then they ate the sacred loaves of bread that only priests are supposed to eat. 5Haven't you read in the Law of Moses that the priests are allowed to work in the temple on the Sabbath? But no one says that they are guilty of breaking the law of the Sabbath. 6I tell you that there is something here greater than the temple. 7Don't you know what the Scriptures mean when they say, "Instead of offering sacrifices to me, I want you to be merciful to others?" If you knew what this means, you would not condemn these innocent disciples of mine. 8So the Son of Man is Lord over the Sabbath.

A Man with a Crippled Hand
(Mark 3.1–6; Luke 6.6–11)

9Jesus left and went into one of the Jewish meeting places, 10where there was a man whose hand was crippled. Some Pharisees wanted to accuse Jesus of doing something wrong, and they asked him, "Is it right to heal someone on the Sabbath?"

11Jesus answered, "If you had a sheep that fell into a ditch on the Sabbath, wouldn't you lift it out? 12People are worth much more than sheep, and so it is right to do good on the Sabbath." 13Then Jesus told the man, "Hold out your hand." The man did, and it became as healthy as the other one.

14The Pharisees left and started making plans to kill Jesus.

God's Chosen Servant

15When Jesus found out what was happening, he left there and large crowds followed him. He healed all of their sick, 16but warned them not to tell anyone about him. 17So God's

---

^{k}*yoke*: Yokes were put on the necks of animals, so that they could pull a plow or wagon. A yoke was a symbol of obedience and hard work. ^{l}*walking through some wheat fields*: It was the custom to let hungry travelers pick grains of wheat.

promise came true, just as Isaiah the prophet had said,

18"Here is my chosen servant!
I love him,
and he pleases me.
I will give him my Spirit,
and he will judge
the nations.
19He will not argue or shout
or be heard speaking
in the streets.
20He will not break off
a bent twig
or put out
a faintly burning flame
until he makes justice
win the victory.
21All nations will place
their hope in him."

Jesus and the Ruler of the Demons
(Mark 3.20–30; Luke 11.14–23;12.10)

22Some people brought to Jesus a man who was blind and could not talk because he had a demon in him. Jesus cured the man, and then he was able to talk and see. 23The crowds were so amazed that they asked, "Could Jesus be the Son of David?"*ᵐ*

24When the Pharisees heard this, they said, "He forces out demons by the power of Beelzebul, the ruler of the demons!"

25Jesus knew what they were thinking, and he said to them:
Any kingdom where people fight each other will end up ruined. And a town or family that fights will soon destroy itself. 26So if Satan fights against himself, how can his kingdom last? 27If I use the power of Beelzebul

to force out demons, whose power do your own followers use to force them out? Your followers are the ones who will judge you. 28But when I force out demons by the power of God's Spirit, it proves that God's kingdom has already come to you. 29How can anyone break into a strong man's house and steal his things, unless he first ties up the strong man? Then he can take everything.

30If you are not on my side, you are against me. If you don't gather in the harvest with me, you scatter it. 31-32I tell you that any sinful thing you do or say can be forgiven. Even if you speak against the Son of Man, you can be forgiven. But if you speak against the Holy Spirit, you can never be forgiven, either in this life or in the life to come.

A Tree and Its Fruit
(Luke 6.43–45)

33A good tree produces only good fruit, and a bad tree produces bad fruit. You can tell what a tree is like by the fruit it produces. 34You are a bunch of evil snakes, so how can you say anything good? Your words show what is in your hearts. 35Good people bring good things out of their hearts, but evil people bring evil things out of their hearts. 36I promise you that on the day of judgment, everyone will have to account for every careless word they have spoken. 37On that day they will be told that they are

---

ᵐCould Jesus be the Son of David: Or "Does Jesus think he is the Son of David?" See the note at 9.27.

either innocent or guilty because of the things they have said.

A Sign from Heaven
(Mark 8.11, 12; Luke 11.29–32)

38Some Pharisees and teachers of the Law of Moses said, "Teacher, we want you to show us a sign from heaven."

39But Jesus replied:

You want a sign because you are evil and won't believe! But the only sign you will get is the sign of the prophet Jonah. 40He was in the stomach of a big fish for three days and nights, just as the Son of Man will be deep in the earth for three days and nights. 41On the day of judgment the people of Nineveh[n] will stand there with you and condemn you. They turned to God when Jonah preached, and yet here is something far greater than Jonah. 42The Queen of the South[o] will also stand there with you and condemn you. She traveled a long way to hear Solomon's wisdom, and yet here is something much greater than Solomon.

Return of an Evil Spirit
(Luke 11.24–26)

43When an evil spirit leaves a person, it travels through the desert, looking for a place to rest. But when the demon doesn't find a place, 44it says, "I will go back to the home I left." When it gets there and finds the place empty, clean, and fixed up, 45it goes off and finds seven other evil spirits even worse than itself. They all come and make their home there, and the person ends up in worse shape than before. That's how it will be with you evil people of today.

Jesus' Mother and Brothers
(Mark 3.31–35; Luke 8.19–21)

46While Jesus was still speaking to the crowds, his mother and brothers came and stood outside because they wanted to talk with him. 47Someone told Jesus, "Your mother and brothers are standing outside and want to talk with you."[p]

48Jesus answered, "Who is my mother and who are my brothers?" 49Then he pointed to his disciples and said, "These are my mother and my brothers! 50Anyone who obeys my Father in heaven is my brother or sister or mother."

A Story about a Farmer
(Mark 4.1–9; Luke 8.4–8)

13 That same day Jesus left the house and went out beside Lake Galilee, where he sat down to teach.[q] 2Such large crowds gathered around him that he had to sit in a boat, while the people stood on the shore.

---

[n]*Nineveh*: During the time of Jonah this city was the capital of the Assyrian Empire, which was Israel's worst enemy. But Jonah was sent there to preach, so that the people would turn to the Lord and be saved.   [o]*Queen of the South*: Sheba, probably a country in southern Arabia.   [p]*with you*: Some manuscripts do not have verse 47.   [q]*sat down to teach*: Teachers in the ancient world, including Jewish teachers, usually sat down when they taught.

Then he taught them many things by using stories. He said:

A farmer went out to scatter seed in a field. 4While the farmer was scattering the seed, some of it fell along the road and was eaten by birds. 5Other seeds fell on thin, rocky ground and quickly started growing because the soil was not very deep. 6But when the sun came up, the plants were scorched and dried up, because they did not have enough roots. 7Some other seeds fell where thorn bushes grew up and choked the plants. 8But a few seeds did fall on good ground where the plants produced a hundred or sixty or thirty times as much as was scattered. 9If you have ears, pay attention!

Why Jesus Used Stories
(Mark 4.10–12; Luke 8.9, 10)

10Jesus' disciples came to him and asked, "Why do you use nothing but stories when you speak to the people?"

11Jesus answered:

I have explained the secrets about the kingdom of heaven to you, but not to others. 12Everyone who has something will be given more. But people who don't have anything will lose even what little they have. 13I use stories when I speak to them because when they look, they cannot see, and when they listen, they cannot hear or understand. 14So God's promise came true, just as the prophet Isaiah had said,

"These people will listen
and listen,
    but never understand.

They will look and look,
    but never see.
15All of them have
    stubborn minds!
Their ears are stopped up,
    and their eyes are covered.
They cannot see or hear
    or understand.
If they could,
they would turn to me,
    and I would heal them."

16But God has blessed you, because your eyes can see and your ears can hear! 17Many prophets and good people were eager to see what you see and to hear what you hear. But I tell you that they did not see or hear.

Jesus Explains the Story about the Farmer
(Mark 4.13–20; Luke 8.11–15)

18Now listen to the meaning of the story about the farmer:

19The seeds that fell along the road are the people who hear the message about the kingdom, but don't understand it. Then the evil one comes and snatches the message from their hearts. 20The seeds that fell on rocky ground are the people who gladly hear the message and accept it right away. 21But they don't have deep roots, and they don't last very long. As soon as life gets hard or the message gets them in trouble, they give up.

22The seeds that fell among the thorn bushes are also people who hear the message. But they start worrying about the needs of this life and are fooled by the desire to get rich. So the message gets choked out, and they never produce anything. 23The seeds that fell on good ground are the people who hear and understand the message. They produce as much as a hundred or sixty or thirty times what was planted.

Weeds among the Wheat

24Jesus then told them this story:

The kingdom of heaven is like what happened when a farmer scattered good seed in a field. 25But while everyone was sleeping, an enemy came and scattered weed seeds in the field and then left.

26When the plants came up and began to ripen, the farmer's servants could see the weeds. 27The servants came and asked, "Sir, didn't you scatter good seed in your field? Where did these weeds come from?"

28"An enemy did this," he replied.

His servants then asked, "Do you want us to go out and pull up the weeds?"

29"No!" he answered. "You might also pull up the wheat. 30Leave the weeds alone until harvest time. Then I'll tell my workers to gather the weeds and tie them up and burn them. But I'll have them store the wheat in my barn."

Stories about a Mustard Seed and Yeast
(Mark 4.30–32; Luke 13.18–21)

31Jesus told them another story:

The kingdom of heaven is like what happens when a farmer plants a mustard seed in a field. 32Although it is the smallest of all seeds, it grows larger than any garden plant and becomes a tree. Birds even come and nest on its branches.

33Jesus also said:

The kingdom of heaven is like what happens when a woman mixes a little yeast into three big batches of flour. Finally, all the dough rises.

The Reason for Teaching with Stories
(Mark 4.33, 34)

34Jesus used stories when he spoke to the people. In fact, he did no tell them anything without using sto ries. 35So God's promise came true just as the prophet[r] had said,

"I will use stories
    to speak my message
and to explain things
    that have been hidden
since the creation
    of the world."

Jesus Explains the Story about the Weeds

36After Jesus left the crowd and went inside,[s] his disciples came to him and said, "Explain to us the story about the weeds in the wheat field."

37Jesus answered:

The one who scattered the good seed is the Son of Man. 38The field is the world, and the good seeds are the people who belong to the kingdom. The weed seeds are those who belong to the

[r]*the prophet*: Some manuscripts have "the prophet Isaiah." [s]*went inside*: Or "went home.'

evil one, 39and the one who scattered them is the devil. The harvest is the end of time, and angels are the ones who bring in the harvest.

40Weeds are gathered and burned. That's how it will be at the end of time. 41The Son of Man will send out his angels, and they will gather from his kingdom everyone who does wrong or causes others to sin. 42Then he will throw them into a flaming furnace, where people will cry and grit their teeth in pain. 43But everyone who has done right will shine like the sun in their Father's kingdom. If you have ears, pay attention!

A Hidden Treasure

44The kingdom of heaven is like what happens when someone finds treasure hidden in a field and buries it again. A person like that is happy and goes and sells everything in order to buy that field.

A Valuable Pearl

45The kingdom of heaven is like what happens when a shop owner is looking for fine pearls. 46After finding a very valuable one, the owner goes and sells everything in order to buy that pearl.

A Fish Net

47The kingdom of heaven is like what happens when a net is thrown into a lake and catches all kinds of fish. 48When the net is full, it is dragged to the shore, and the fishermen sit down to separate the fish. They keep the good ones, but throw the bad ones away. 49That's how it will be at the end of time. Angels will come and separate the evil people from the ones who have done right. 50Then those evil people will be thrown into a flaming furnace, where they will cry and grit their teeth in pain.

New and Old Treasures

51Jesus asked his disciples if they understood all these things. They said, "Yes, we do."

52So he told them, "Every student of the Scriptures who becomes a disciple in the kingdom of heaven is like someone who brings out new and old treasures from the storeroom."

The People of Nazareth Turn against Jesus
(Mark 6.1–6; Luke 4.16–30)

53When Jesus had finished telling these stories, he left 54and went to his hometown. He taught in their meeting place, and the people were so amazed that they asked, "Where does he get all this wisdom and the power to work these miracles? 55Isn't he the son of the carpenter? Isn't Mary his mother, and aren't James, Joseph, Simon, and Judas his brothers? 56Don't his sisters still live here in our town? How can he do all this?" 57So the people were very unhappy because of what he was doing.

But Jesus said, "Prophets are honored by everyone, except the people of their hometown and their own family." 58And because the people did not have any faith, Jesus did not work many miracles there.

The Death of John the Baptist
(Mark 6.14–29; Luke 9.7–9)

14 About this time Herod the ruler*t* heard the news about Jesus ²and told his officials, "This is John the Baptist! He has come back from death, and that's why he has the power to work these miracles."

³⁻⁴Herod had earlier arrested John and had him chained and put in prison. He did this because John had told him, "It isn't right for you to take Herodias, the wife of your brother Philip." ⁵Herod wanted to kill John. But the people thought John was a prophet, and Herod was afraid of what they might do.

⁶When Herod's birthday came, the daughter of Herodias danced for the guests. She pleased Herod ⁷so much that he swore to give her whatever she wanted. ⁸But the girl's mother told her to say, "Here on a platter I want the head of John the Baptist!"

⁹The king was sorry for what he had said. But he did not want to break the promise he had made in front of his guests. So he ordered a guard ¹⁰to go to the prison and cut off John's head. ¹¹It was taken on a platter to the girl, and she gave it to her mother. ¹²John's followers took his body and buried it. Then they told Jesus what had happened.

Jesus Feeds Five Thousand
(Mark 6.30–44; Luke 9.10–17; John 6.1–14)

¹³After Jesus heard about John, he crossed Lake Galilee*u* to go to some place where he could be alone. But the crowds found out and followed him on foot from the towns. ¹⁴When Jesus got out of the boat, he saw the large crowd. He felt sorry for them and healed everyone who was sick.

¹⁵That evening the disciples came to Jesus and said, "This place is like a desert, and it is already late. Let the crowds leave, so they can go to the villages and buy some food."

¹⁶Jesus replied, "They don't have to leave. Why don't you give them something to eat?"

¹⁷But they said, "We have only five small loaves of bread*v* and two fish."

¹⁸Jesus asked his disciples to bring the food to him, ¹⁹and he told the crowd to sit down on the grass. Jesus took the five loaves and the two fish. He looked up toward heaven and blessed the food. Then he broke the bread and handed it to his disciples, and they gave it to the people.

²⁰After everyone had eaten all they wanted, Jesus' disciples picked up twelve large baskets of leftovers. ²¹There were about five thousand men who ate, not counting the women and children.

Jesus Walks on the Water
(Mark 6.45–52; John 6.15–21)

²²Right away Jesus made his disciples get into a boat and start back across the lake.*w* But he stayed until he had sent the crowds away. ²³Then he went up on a mountain where he could be alone and pray. Later that evening, he was still there.

²⁴By this time the boat was a long

---

t Herod the ruler: Herod Antipas, the son of Herod the Great (2.1). *u crossed Lake Galilee*: To the east side. *v small loaves of bread*: These would have been flat and round or in the shape of a bun. *w back across the lake*: To the west side.

way from the shore. It was going against the wind and was being tossed around by the waves. 25A little while before morning, Jesus came walking on the water toward his disciples. 26When they saw him, they thought he was a ghost. They were terrified and started screaming.

27At once Jesus said to them, "Don't worry! I am Jesus. Don't be afraid."

28Peter replied, "Lord, if it is really you, tell me to come to you on the water."

29"Come on!" Jesus said. Peter then got out of the boat and started walking on the water toward him.

30But when Peter saw how strong the wind was, he was afraid and started sinking. "Lord, save me!" he shouted.

31Right away Jesus reached out his hand. He helped Peter up and said, "You surely don't have much faith. Why do you doubt?"

32When Jesus and Peter got into the boat, the wind died down. 33The men in the boat worshiped Jesus and said, "You really are the Son of God!"

Jesus Heals Sick People in Gennesaret
(Mark 6.53–56)

34Jesus and his disciples crossed the lake and came to shore near the town of Gennesaret. 35The people found out that he was there, and they sent word to everyone who lived in that part of the country. So they brought all the sick people to Jesus. 36They begged him just to let them touch his clothes, and everyone who did was healed.

The Teaching of the Ancestors
(Mark 7.1–13)

15 About this time some Pharisees and teachers of the Law of Moses came from Jerusalem. They asked Jesus, 2"Why don't your disciples obey what our ancestors taught us to do? They don't even wash their hands^x before they eat."

3Jesus answered:

Why do you disobey God and follow your own teaching? 4Didn't God command you to respect your father and mother? Didn't he tell you to put to death all who curse their parents? 5But you let people get by without helping their parents when they should. You let them say that what they have has been offered to God.^{y} 6Is this any way to show respect to your parents? You ignore God's commands in order to follow your own teaching. 7And you are nothing but showoffs! Isaiah the prophet was right when he wrote that God had said,

8"All of you praise me
    with your words,
but you never really
    think about me.
9It is useless for you
    to worship me,
when you teach rules
    made up by humans."

---

^{x}*wash their hands*: The Jewish people had strict laws about washing their hands before eating, especially if they had been out in public. ^{y}*has been offered to God*: According to Jewish custom, when people said something was offered to God, it belonged to him and could not be used for anyone else, not even for their own parents.

What Really Makes People Unclean
(Mark 7.14–23)

10Jesus called the crowd together and said, "Pay attention and try to understand what I mean. 11The food that you put into your mouth doesn't make you unclean and unfit to worship God. The bad words that come out of your mouth are what make you unclean."

12Then his disciples came over to him and asked, "Do you know that you insulted the Pharisees by what you said?"

13Jesus answered, "Every plant that my Father in heaven did not plant will be pulled up by the roots. 14Stay away from those Pharisees! They are like blind people leading other blind people, and all of them will fall into a ditch."

15Peter replied, "What did you mean when you talked about the thi gs that make people unclean?"

16Jesus then said:

Don't any of you know what I am talking about by now? 17Don't you know that the food you put into your mouth goes into your stomach and then out of your body? 18But the words that come out of your mouth come from your heart. And they are what make you unfit to worship God. 19Out of your heart come evil thoughts, murder, unfaithfulness in marriage, vulgar deeds, stealing, telling lies, and insulting others. 20These are what make you unclean. Eating without washing your hands will not make you unfit to worship God.

A Woman's Faith
(Mark 7.24–30)

21Jesus left and went to the territory near the cities of Tyre and Sidon. 22Suddenly a Canaanite woman[z] from there came out shouting, "Lord and Son of David,[a] have pity on me! My daughter is full of demons." 23Jesus did not say a word. But the woman kept following along and shouting, so his disciples came up and asked him to send her away.

24Jesus said, "I was sent only to the people of Israel! They are like a flock of lost sheep."

25The woman came closer. Then she kneeled down and begged, "Lord, please help me!"

26Jesus replied, "It isn't right to take food away from children and feed it to dogs."[b]

27"Lord, that's true," the woman said, "but even dogs get the crumbs that fall from their owner's table."

28Jesus answered, "Dear woman, you really do have a lot of faith, and you will be given what you want." At that moment her daughter was healed.

Jesus Heals Many People

29From there Jesus went along Lake Galilee. Then he climbed a hill and sat down. 30Large crowds came and brought many people who were crippled or blind or lame or unable to talk. They placed them, and many others, in front of Jesus, and he healed them all. 31Everyone was amazed at what they saw and heard. People who had never spoken could now speak. The lame were healed. The crippled

---

[z]Canaanite woman: This woman was not Jewish.   [a]Son of David: See the note at 9.27.   [b]feed it to dogs: The Jewish people sometimes referred to Gentiles as dogs.

could walk, and the blind were able to see. Everyone was praising the God of Israel.

Jesus Feeds Four Thousand
(Mark 8.1–10)

32Jesus called his disciples together and told them, "I feel sorry for these people. They have been with me for three days, and they don't have anything to eat. I don't want to send them away hungry. They might faint on their way home."

33His disciples said, "This place is like a desert. Where can we find enough food to feed such a crowd?"

34Jesus asked them how much food they had. They replied, "Seven small loaves of bread*c* and a few little fish."

35After Jesus had told the people to sit down, **36**he took the seven loaves of bread and the fish and gave thanks. He then broke them and handed them to his disciples, who passed them around to the crowds.

37Everyone ate all they wanted, and the leftovers filled seven large baskets. **38**There were four thousand men who ate, not counting the women and children.

39After Jesus had sent the crowds away, he got into a boat and sailed across the lake. He came to shore near the town of Magadan.*d*

A Demand for a Sign from Heaven
(Mark 8.11–13; Luke 12.54–56)

16 The Pharisees and Sadducees came to Jesus and tried to test him by asking for a sign from heaven. **2**He told them:

If the sky is red in the evening, you say the weather will be good. **3**But if the sky is red and gloomy in the morning, you say it is going to rain. You can tell what the weather will be like by looking at the sky. But you don't understand what is happening now.*e* **4**You want a sign because you are evil and won't believe! But the only sign you will be given is what happened to Jonah.*f*

Then Jesus left.

The Yeast of the Pharisees and Sadducees
(Mark 8.14–21)

5The disciples had forgotten to bring any bread when they crossed the lake.*g* **6**Jesus then warned them, "Watch out! Guard against the yeast of the Pharisees and Sadducees."

7The disciples talked this over and said to each other, "He must be saying this because we didn't bring along any bread."

8Jesus knew what they were thinking and said:

You surely don't have much faith! Why are you talking about not having any bread? **9**Don't you understand? Have you forgotten about the five thousand people and all those baskets of leftovers from just five loaves of bread? **10**And what about the four thousand people and all those baskets

---

small loaves of bread: See the note at 14.17.   *dMagadan*: The location is unknown.   *eIf the sky is red . . . what is happening now*: The words of Jesus in verses 2 and 3 are not in some manuscripts.   *fwhat happened to Jonah*: Jonah was in the stomach of a big fish for three days and nights. See 12.40.   *gcrossed the lake*: To the east side.

of leftovers from only seven loaves of bread? 11Don't you know by now that I am not talking to you about bread? Watch out for the yeast of the Pharisees and Sadducees!

12Finally, the disciples understood that Jesus was not talking about the yeast used to make bread, but about the teaching of the Pharisees and Sadducees.

Who Is Jesus?
(Mark 8.27–30; Luke 9.18–21)

13When Jesus and his disciples were near the town of Caesarea Philippi, he asked them, "What do people say about the Son of Man?"

14The disciples answered, "Some people say you are John the Baptist or maybe Elijah*h* or Jeremiah or some other prophet."

15Then Jesus asked them, "But who do you say I am?"

16Simon Peter spoke up, "You are the Messiah, the Son of the living God."

17Jesus told him:

Simon, son of Jonah, you are blessed! You didn't discover this on your own. It was shown to you by my Father in heaven. 18So I will call you Peter, which means "a rock." On this rock I will build my church, and death itself will not have any power over it. 19I will give you the keys to the kingdom of heaven, and God in heaven will allow whatever you allow on earth. But he will not allow anything that you don't allow.

20Jesus told his disciples not to tell anyone that he was the Messiah.

Jesus Speaks about His Suffering and Death
(Mark 8.31—9.1; Luke 9.22–27)

21From then on, Jesus began telling his disciples what would happen to him. He said, "I must go to Jerusalem. There the nation's leaders, the chief priests, and the teachers of the Law of Moses will make me suffer terribly. I will be killed, but three days later I will rise to life."

22Peter took Jesus aside and told him to stop talking like that. He said, "Lord, surely God won't let this happen to you!"

23Jesus turned to Peter and said, "Satan, get away from me! You're in my way because you think like everyone else and not like God."

24Then Jesus said to his disciples:

If any of you want to be my followers, you must forget about yourself. You must take up your cross and follow me. 25If you want to save your life,*i* you will destroy it. But if you give up your life for me, you will find it. 26What will you gain, if you own the whole world but destroy yourself? What would you give to get back your soul?

27The Son of Man will soon come in the glory of his Father and with his angels to reward all people for what they have done. 28I promise you that some of those standing here will not die

---

hElijah: Many of the Jewish people expected the prophet Elijah to come and prepare the way for the Messiah.   *ilife*: In verses 25 and 26 the same Greek word is translated "life," "yourself," and "soul."

before they see the Son of Man coming with his kingdom.

The True Glory of Jesus
(Mark 9.2–13; Luke 9.28–36)

17 Six days later Jesus took Peter and the brothers James and John with him. They went up on a very high mountain where they could be alone. ²There in front of the disciples Jesus was completely changed. His face was shining like the sun, and his clothes became white as light.

³All at once Moses and Elijah were there talking with Jesus. ⁴So Peter said to him, "Lord, it is good for us to be here! Let us make three shelters, one for you, one for Moses, and one for Elijah."

⁵While Peter was still speaking, the shadow of a bright cloud passed over them. From the cloud a voice said, "This is my own dear Son, and I am pleased with him. Listen to what he says!" ⁶When the disciples heard the voice, they were so afraid that they fell flat on the ground. ⁷But Jesus came over and touched them. He said, "Get up and don't be afraid!" ⁸When they opened their eyes, they saw only Jesus.

⁹On their way down from the mountain, Jesus warned his disciples not to tell anyone what they had seen until after the Son of Man had been raised from death.

¹⁰The disciples asked Jesus, "Don't the teachers of the Law of Moses say that Elijah must come before the Messiah does?"

¹¹Jesus told them, "Elijah certainly will come and get everything ready. ¹²In fact, he has already come.

But the people did not recognize him and treated him just as they wanted to. They will soon make the Son of Man suffer in the same way." ¹³Then the disciples understood that Jesus was talking to them about John the Baptist.

Jesus Heals a Boy
(Mark 9.14–29; Luke 9.37–43a)

¹⁴Jesus and his disciples returned to the crowd. A man kneeled in front of him ¹⁵and said, "Lord, have pity on my son! He has a bad case of epilepsy and often falls into a fire or into water. ¹⁶I brought him to your disciples, but none of them could heal him."

¹⁷Jesus said, "You people are too stubborn to have any faith! How much longer must I be with you? Why do I have to put up with you? Bring the boy here." ¹⁸Then Jesus spoke sternly to the demon. It went out of the boy, and right then he was healed.

¹⁹Later the disciples went to Jesus in private and asked him, "Why couldn't we force out the demon?"

²⁰⁻²¹Jesus replied:

It is because you don't have enough faith! But I can promise you this. If you had faith no larger than a mustard seed, you could tell this mountain to move from here to there. And it would. Everything would be possible for you.*ʲ*

Jesus Again Speaks about His Death
(Mark 9.30–32; Luke 9.43b–45)

²²While Jesus and his disciples were going from place to place in

---

ʲor you: Some manuscripts add, "But the only way to force out that kind of demon is by praying and going without eating."

Galilee, he told them, "The Son of Man will be handed over to people 23who will kill him. But three days later he will rise to life." All of this made the disciples very sad.

Paying the Temple Tax

24When Jesus and the others arrived in Capernaum, the collectors for the temple tax came to Peter and asked, "Does your teacher pay the temple tax?"

25"Yes, he does," Peter answered.

After they had returned home, Jesus went up to Peter and asked him, "Simon, what do you think? Do the kings of this earth collect taxes and fees from their own people or from foreigners?"[k]

26Peter answered, "From foreigners."

Jesus replied, "Then their own people[l] don't have to pay. 27But we don't want to cause trouble. So go cast a line into the lake and pull out the first fish you hook. Open its mouth, and you will find a coin. Use it to pay your taxes and mine."

Who Is the Greatest?
(Mark 9.33–37; Luke 9.46–48)

18 About this time, the disciples came to Jesus and asked him who would be the greatest in the kingdom of heaven. 2Jesus called a child over and had the child stand near him. 3Then he said:

I promise you this. If you don't change and become like this child, you will never get into the kingdom of heaven. 4But if you are as humble as this child, you are the greatest in the kingdom of heaven. 5And when you welcome one of these children because of me, you welcome me.

Temptations to Sin
(Mark 9.42–48; Luke 17.1, 2)

6It will be terrible for people who cause even one of my little followers to sin. Those people would be better off thrown into the deepest part of the ocean with a heavy stone tied around the neck! 7The world is in for trouble because of the way it causes people to sin. There will always be something to cause people to sin, but anyone who does this will be in for trouble.

8If your hand or foot causes you to sin, chop it off and throw it away! You would be better off to go into life crippled or lame than to have two hands or two feet and be thrown into the fire that never goes out. 9If your eye causes you to sin, poke it out and get rid of it. You would be better off to go into life with only one eye than to have two eyes and be thrown into the fires of hell.

The Lost Sheep
(Luke 15.3–7)

10-11Don't be cruel to any of these little ones! I promise you that their angels are always with my Father in heaven."[m] 12Let me

---

[k]*from their own people or from foreigners*: Or "from their children or from others." [l]*From foreigners . . . their own people*: Or "From other people . . . their children." [m]*in heaven* Some manuscripts add, "The Son of Man came to save people who are lost."

ask you this. What would you do if you had a hundred sheep and one of them wandered off? Wouldn't you leave the ninety-nine on the hillside and go look for the one that had wandered away? 13I am sure that finding it would make you happier than having the ninety-nine that never wandered off. 14That's how it is with your Father in heaven. He doesn't want any of these little ones to be lost.

When Someone Sins
(Luke 17.3)

15If one of my followers[n] sins against you, go and point out what was wrong. But do it in private, just between the two of you. If that person listens, you have won back a follower. 16But if that one refuses to listen, take along one or two others. The Scriptures teach that every complaint must be proven true by two or more witnesses. 17If the follower refuses to listen to them, report the matter to the church. Anyone who refuses to listen to the church must be treated like an unbeliever or a tax collector.[o]

Allowing and Not Allowing

18I promise you that God in heaven will allow whatever you allow on earth, but he will not allow anything you don't allow. 19I promise that when any two of you

on earth agree about something you are praying for, my Father in heaven will do it for you. 20Whenever two or three of you come together in my name,[p] I am there with you.

An Official Who Refused to Forgive

21Peter came up to the Lord and asked, "How many times should I forgive someone[q] who does something wrong to me? Is seven times enough?"
22Jesus answered:

Not just seven times, but seventy-seven times![r] 23This story will show you what the kingdom of heaven is like:

One day a king decided to call in his officials and ask them to give an account of what they owed him. 24As he was doing this, one official was brought in who owed him fifty million silver coins. 25But he didn't have any money to pay what he owed. The king ordered him to be sold, along with his wife and children and all he owned, in order to pay the debt.

26The official got down on his knees and began begging, "Have pity on me, and I will pay you every cent I owe!" 27The king felt sorry for him and let him go free. He even told the official that he did not have to pay back the money.

28As the official was leaving, he happened to meet another official, who owed him a hundred

---

[n]followers: The Greek text has "brother," which is used here and elsewhere in this chapter to refer to a follower of Christ. [o]tax collector: See the note at 5.46. [p]in my name: Or "as my followers." [q]someone: Or "a follower." See the note at 18.15. [r]seventy-seven times: Or "seventy times seven." The large number means that one follower should never stop forgiving another.

silver coins. So he grabbed the man by the throat. He started choking him and said, "Pay me what you owe!"

29The man got down on his knees and began begging, "Have pity on me, and I will pay you back." **30**But the first official refused to have pity. Instead, he went and had the other official put in jail until he could pay what he owed.

31When some other officials found out what had happened, they felt sorry for the man who had been put in jail. Then they told the king what had happened. **32**The king called the first official back in and said, "You're an evil man! When you begged for mercy, I said you did not have to pay back a cent. **33**Don't you think you should show pity to someone else, as I did to you?" **34**The king was so angry that he ordered the official to be tortured until he could pay back everything he owed. **35**That is how my Father in heaven will treat you, if you don't forgive each of my followers with all your heart.

Teaching about Divorce
(Mark 10.1–12)

19 When Jesus finished teaching, he left Galilee and went to the part of Judea that is east of the Jordan River. **2**Large crowds followed him, and he healed their sick people.

3Some Pharisees wanted to test Jesus. They came up to him and asked, "Is it right for a man to divorce his wife for just any reason?"

4Jesus answered, "Don't you know that in the beginning the Creator made a man and a woman? **5**That's why a man leaves his father and mother and gets married. He becomes like one person with his wife. **6**Then they are no longer two people, but one. And no one should separate a couple that God has joined together."

7The Pharisees asked Jesus, "Why did Moses say that a man could write out divorce papers and send his wife away?"

8Jesus replied, "You are so heartless! That's why Moses allowed you to divorce your wife. But from the beginning God did not intend it to be that way. **9**I say that if your wife has not committed some terrible sexual sin,§ you must not divorce her to marry someone else. If you do, you are unfaithful."

10The disciples said, "If that's how it is between a man and a woman, it's better not to get married."

11Jesus told them, "Only those people who have been given the gift of staying single can accept this teaching. **12**Some people are unable to marry because of birth defects or because of what someone has done to their bodies. Others stay single for the sake of the kingdom of heaven. Anyone who can accept this teaching should do so."

Jesus Blesses Little Children
(Mark 10.13–16; Luke 18.15–17)

13Some people brought their children to Jesus, so that he could place his hands on them and pray for them. His disciples told the people to stop bothering him. **14**But Jesus said, "Let the children come to me, and don't try

---

§*some terrible sexual sin*: See the note at 5.32.

to stop them! People who are like these children belong to God's kingdom."*t* 15After Jesus had placed his hands on the children, he left.

A Rich Young Man
(Mark 10.17–31; Luke 18.18–30)

16A man came to Jesus and asked, "Teacher, what good thing must I do to have eternal life?"

17Jesus said to him, "Why do you ask me about what is good? Only God is good. If you want to have eternal life, you must obey his commandments."

18"Which ones?" the man asked.

Jesus answered, "Do not murder. Be faithful in marriage. Do not steal. Do not tell lies about others. 19Respect your father and mother. And love others as much as you love yourself."

20The young man said, "I have obeyed all of these. What else must I do?"

21Jesus replied, "If you want to be perfect, go sell everything you own! Give the money to the poor, and you will have riches in heaven. Then come and be my follower." 22When the young man heard this, he was sad, because he was very rich.

23Jesus said to his disciples, "It's terribly hard for rich people to get into the kingdom of heaven! 24In fact, it's easier for a camel to go through the eye of a needle than for a rich person to get into God's kingdom."

25When the disciples heard this, they were greatly surprised and asked, "How can anyone ever be saved?"

26Jesus looked straight at them and said, "There are some things that people cannot do, but God can do anything."

27Peter replied, "Remember, we have left everything to be your followers! What will we get?"

28Jesus answered:

Yes, all of you have become my followers. And so in the future world, when the Son of Man sits on his glorious throne, I promise that you will sit on twelve thrones to judge the twelve tribes of Israel. 29All who have given up home or brothers and sisters or father and mother or children or land for me will be given a hundred times as much. They will also have eternal life. 30But many who are now first will be last, and many who are last will be first.

Workers in a Vineyard

20 As Jesus was telling what the kingdom of heaven would be like, he said:

Early one morning a man went out to hire some workers for his vineyard. 2After he had agreed to pay them the usual amount for a day's work, he sent them off to his vineyard.

3About nine that morning, the man saw some other people standing in the market with nothing to do. 4He said he would pay them what was fair, if they would work in his vineyard. 5So they went.

At noon and again about three in the afternoon he returned to the market. And each time he made the same agreement with others who were loafing around with nothing to do.

People who are like these children belong to God's kingdom: Or "God's kingdom belongs to people who are like these children."

6Finally, about five in the afternoon the man went back and found some others standing there. He asked them, "Why have you been standing here all day long doing nothing?"

7"Because no one has hired us," they answered. Then he told them to go work in his vineyard.

8That evening the owner of the vineyard told the man in charge of the workers to call them in and give them their money. He also told the man to begin with the ones who were hired last. 9When the workers arrived, the ones who had been hired at five in the afternoon were given a full day's pay.

10The workers who had been hired first thought they would be given more than the others. But when they were given the same, 11they began complaining to the owner of the vineyard. 12They said, "The ones who were hired last worked for only one hour. But you paid them the same that you did us. And we worked in the hot sun all day long!"

13The owner answered one of them, "Friend, I didn't cheat you. I paid you exactly what we agreed on. 14Take your money now and go! What business is it of yours if I want to pay them the same that I paid you? 15Don't I have the right to do what I want with my own money? Why should you be jealous, if I want to be generous?"

16Jesus then said, "So it is. Everyone who is now first will be last, and everyone who is last will be first."

Jesus Again Tells about His Death
(Mark 10.32–34; Luke 18.31–34)

17As Jesus was on his way to Jerusalem, he took his twelve disciples aside and told them in private:

18We are now on our way to Jerusalem, where the Son of Man will be handed over to the chief priests and the teachers of the Law of Moses. They will sentence him to death, 19and then they will hand him over to foreigners^u who will make fun of him. They will beat him and nail him to a cross. But on the third day he will rise from death.

A Mother's Request
(Mark 10.35–45)

20The mother of James and John^v came to Jesus with her two sons. She kneeled down and started begging him to do something for her. 21Jesus asked her what she wanted, and she said, "When you come into your kingdom please let one of my sons sit at your right side and the other at your left."^{u}

22Jesus answered, "Not one of you knows what you are asking. Are you able to drink from the cup^x that I must soon drink from?"

James and John said, "Yes we are!"

---

^{u}*foreigners*: The Romans, who ruled Judea at this time. ^{v}*mother of James and John*: The Greek text has "mother of the sons of Zebedee." See 26.37. ^{w}*right side . . . left*: The most powerful people in a kingdom sat at the right and left side of the king. ^{x}*drink from the cup*: In the Scriptures a cup is sometimes used as a symbol of suffering. To "drink from the cup" is to suffer.

23Jesus replied, "You certainly will drink from my cup! But it is not for me to say who will sit at my right side and at my left. That is for my Father to say."

24When the ten other disciples heard this, they were angry with the two brothers. 25But Jesus called the disciples together and said:

You know that foreign rulers like to order their people around. And their great leaders have full power over everyone they rule. 26But don't act like them. If you want to be great, you must be the servant of all the others. 27And if you want to be first, you must be the slave of the rest. 28The Son of Man did not come to be a slave master, but a slave who will give his life to rescue*y* many people.

Jesus Heals Two Blind Men
(Mark 10.46–52; Luke 18.35–43)

29Jesus was followed by a large crowd as he and his disciples were leaving Jericho. 30Two blind men were sitting beside the road. And when they heard that Jesus was coming their way, they shouted, "Lord and Son of David,*z* have pity on us!"

31The crowd told them to be quiet, but they shouted even louder, "Lord and Son of David, have pity on us!"

32When Jesus heard them, he stopped and asked, "What do you want me to do for you?"

33They answered, "Lord, we want to see!"

34Jesus felt sorry for them and touched their eyes. Right away they could see, and they became his followers.

Jesus Enters Jerusalem
(Mark 11.1–11; Luke 19.28–38;
John 12.12–19)

21 When Jesus and his disciples came near to Jerusalem, he went to Bethphage on the Mount of Olives and sent two of them on ahead. 2He told them, "Go into the next village, where you will at once find a donkey and her colt. Untie the two donkeys and bring them to me. 3If anyone asks why you are doing that, just say, 'The Lord*a* needs them.' Right away he will let you have the donkeys."

4So God's promise came true, just as the prophet had said,

5"Announce to the people
of Jerusalem:
'Your king is coming to you!
He is humble
and rides on a donkey.
He comes on the colt
of a donkey.' "

6The disciples left and did what Jesus had told them to do. 7They brought the donkey and its colt and laid some clothes on their backs. Then Jesus got on.

8Many people spread clothes in the road, while others put down branches*b* which they had cut from trees. 9Some people walked ahead of Jesus and others followed behind. They were all shouting,

---

*y*rescue: The Greek word often, though not always, means the payment of a price to free a slave or a prisoner.   *z*Son of David: See the note at 9.27.   *a*The Lord: Or "the master of the donkeys."   *b*spread clothes . . . put down branches: This was one way that the Jewish people welcomed a famous person.

"Hooray[c] for the Son of David![d]
God bless the one who comes
   in the name of the Lord.
Hooray for God
   in heaven above!"

10When Jesus came to Jerusalem, everyone in the city was excited and asked, "Who can this be?"

11The crowd answered, "This is Jesus, the prophet from Nazareth in Galilee."

Jesus in the Temple
(Mark 11.15–19; Luke 19.45–48; John 2.13–22)

12Jesus went into the temple and chased out everyone who was selling or buying. He turned over the tables of the moneychangers and the benches of the ones who were selling doves. 13He told them, "The Scriptures say, 'My house should be called a place of worship.' But you have turned it into a place where robbers hide."

14Blind and lame people came to Jesus in the temple, and he healed them. 15But the chief priests and the teachers of the Law of Moses were angry when they saw his miracles and heard the children shouting praises to the Son of David.[d] 16The men said to Jesus, "Don't you hear what those children are saying?"

"Yes, I do!" Jesus answered. "Don't you know that the Scriptures say, 'Children and infants will sing praises'?"

17Then Jesus left the city and went out to the village of Bethany, where he spent the night.

Jesus Puts a Curse on a Fig Tree
(Mark 11.12–14, 20–24)

18When Jesus got up the next morning, he was hungry. He started out for the city, 19and along the way he saw a fig tree. But when he came to it, he found only leaves and no figs. So he told the tree, "You will never again grow any fruit!" Right then the fig tree dried up.

20The disciples were shocked when they saw how quickly the tree had dried up. 21But Jesus said to them, "If you have faith and don't doubt, I promise that you can do what I did to this tree. And you will be able to do even more. You can tell this mountain to get up and jump into the sea, and it will. 22If you have faith when you pray, you will be given whatever you ask for."

A Question about Jesus' Authority
(Mark 11.27–33; Luke 20.1–8)

23Jesus had gone into the temple and was teaching when the chief priests and the leaders of the people came up to him. They asked, "What right do you have to do these things? Who gave you this authority?"

24Jesus answered, "I have just one question to ask you. If you answer it, I will tell you where I got the right to do these things. 25Who gave John the right to baptize? Was it God in heaven or merely some human being?"

They thought it over and said to each other, "We can't say that God gave John this right. Jesus will ask us why we didn't believe John. 26On the other hand, these people think that

---

[c]*Hooray*: This translates a word that can mean "please save us." But it is most often used as a shout of praise to God.   [d]*Son of David*: See the note at 9.27.

John was a prophet, and we are afraid of what they might do to us. That's why we can't say that it was merely some human who gave John the right to baptize." 27So they told Jesus, "We don't know."

Jesus said, "Then I won't tell you who gave me the right to do what I do."

A Story about Two Sons

28Jesus said:

I will tell you a story about a man who had two sons. Then you can tell me what you think. The father went to the older son and said, "Go work in the vineyard today!" 29His son told him that he would not do it, but later he changed his mind and went. 30The man then told his younger son to go work in the vineyard. The boy said he would, but he didn't go. 31Which one of the sons obeyed his father?

"The older one," the chief priests and leaders answered.

Then Jesus told them:

You can be sure that tax collectors*ᵉ* and bad women will get into the kingdom of God before you ever will! 32When John the Baptist showed you how to do right, you would not believe him. But these evil people did believe. And even when you saw what they did, you still would not change your minds and believe.

Renters of a Vineyard
(Mark 12.1–12; Luke 20.9–19)

33Jesus told the chief priests and leaders to listen to this story:

A land owner once planted a vineyard. He built a wall around it and dug a pit to crush the grapes in. He also built a lookout tower. Then he rented out his vineyard and left the country.

34When it was harvest time, the owner sent some servants to get his share of the grapes. 35But the renters grabbed those servants. They beat up one, killed one, and stoned one of them to death. 36He then sent more servants than he did the first time. But the renters treated them in the same way.

37Finally, the owner sent his own son to the renters, because he thought they would respect him. 38But when they saw the man's son, they said, "Someday he will own the vineyard. Let's kill him! Then we can have it all for ourselves." 39So they grabbed him, threw him out of the vineyard, and killed him.

40Jesus asked, "When the owner of that vineyard comes, what do you suppose he will do to those renters?"

41The chief priests and leaders answered, "He will kill them in some horrible way. Then he will rent out his vineyard to people who will give him his share of grapes at harvest time."

42Jesus replied, "Surely you know that the Scriptures say,

'The stone that the builders
     tossed aside
is now the most important
     stone of all.
This is something
the Lord has done,
     and it is amazing to us.'

ᵉtax collectors: See the note at 5.46.

43I tell you that God's kingdom will be taken from you and given to people who will do what he demands. 44Anyone who stumbles over this stone will be crushed, and anyone it falls on will be smashed to pieces."*f*

45When the chief priests and the Pharisees heard these stories, they knew that Jesus was talking about them. 46They looked for a way to kill him. But they were afraid to arrest Jesus, because the people thought he was a prophet.

The Great Banquet
(Luke 14.15–24)

22 Once again Jesus used stories to teach the people:

2The kingdom of heaven is like what happened when a king gave a wedding banquet for his son. 3The king sent some servants to tell the invited guests to come to the banquet, but the guests refused. 4He sent other servants to say to the guests, "The banquet is ready! My cattle and prize calves have all been prepared. Everything is ready. Come to the banquet!"

5But the guests did not pay any attention. Some of them left for their farms, and some went to their places of business. 6Others grabbed the servants, beat them up, and killed them.

7This made the king so furious that he sent an army to kill those murderers and burn down their city. 8Then he said to the servants, "It is time for the wedding banquet, and the invited guests don't deserve to come. 9Go out to the street corners and tell everyone you meet to come to the banquet." 10They went out on the streets and brought in everyone they could find, good and bad alike. And the banquet room was filled with guests.

11When the king went in to meet the guests, he found that one of them was not wearing the right kind of clothes for the wedding. 12The king asked, "Friend, why didn't you wear proper clothes for the wedding?" But the guest had no excuse. 13So the king gave orders for that person to be tied hand and foot and to be thrown outside into the dark. That's where people will cry and grit their teeth in pain. 14Many are invited, but only a few are chosen.

Paying Taxes
(Mark 12.13–17; Luke 20.20–26)

15The Pharisees got together and planned how they could trick Jesus into saying something wrong. 16They sent some of their followers and some of Herod's followers*g* to say to him, "Teacher, we know that you are honest. You teach the truth about what God wants people to do. And you treat everyone with the same respect, no matter who they are. 17Tell us what you think! Should we pay taxes to the Emperor or not?"

18Jesus knew their evil thoughts and said, "Why are you trying to test

---

f pieces: Verse 44 is not in some manuscripts.　　*g Herod's followers*: People who were political followers of the family of Herod the Great (2.1) and his son Herod Antipas (14.1), and who wanted Herod to be king in Jerusalem.

me? You showoffs! ¹⁹Let me see one of the coins used for paying taxes." They brought him a silver coin, ²⁰and he asked, "Whose picture and name are on it?"

²¹"The Emperor's," they answered.

Then Jesus told them, "Give the Emperor what belongs to him and give God what belongs to God." ²²His answer surprised them so much that they walked away.

Life in the Future World
(Mark 12.18–27; Luke 20.27–40)

²³The Sadducees did not believe that people would rise to life after death. So that same day some of the Sadducees came to Jesus and said:

²⁴Teacher, Moses wrote that if a married man dies and has no children, his brother should marry the widow. Their first son would then be thought of as the son of the dead brother. ²⁵Once there were seven brothers who lived here. The first one married, but died without having any children. So his wife was left to his brother. ²⁶The same thing happened to the second and third brothers and finally to all seven of them. ²⁷At last the woman died. ²⁸When God raises people from death, whose wife will this woman be? She had been married to all seven brothers. ²⁹Jesus answered:

You are completely wrong! You don't know what the Scriptures teach. And you don't know any-

thing about the power of God. ³⁰When God raises people to life, they won't marry. They will be like the angels in heaven. ³¹And as for people being raised to life, God was speaking to you when he said, ³²"I am the God worshiped by Abraham, Isaac, and Jacob."*ʰ* He is not the God of the dead, but of the living.

³³The crowds were surprised to hear what Jesus was teaching.

The Most Important Commandment
(Mark 12.28–34; Luke 10.25–28)

³⁴After Jesus had made the Sadducees look foolish, the Pharisees heard about it and got together. ³⁵One of them was an expert in the Jewish Law. So he tried to test Jesus by asking, ³⁶"Teacher, what is the most important commandment in the Law?"

³⁷Jesus answered:

Love the Lord your God with all your heart, soul, and mind. ³⁸This is the first and most important commandment. ³⁹The second most important commandment is like this one. And it is, "Love others as much as you love yourself." ⁴⁰All the Law of Moses and the Books of the Prophets*ⁱ* are based on these two commandments.

About David's Son
(Mark 12.35–37; Luke 20.41–44)

⁴¹While the Pharisees were still there, Jesus asked them, ⁴²"What do

---

ʰI am the God worshiped by Abraham, Isaac, and Jacob: Jesus argues that if God is worshiped by these three, they must still be alive, because he is the God of the living. *ⁱthe Law of Moses and the Books of the Prophets:* The Jewish Scriptures, that is, the Old Testament.

you think about the Messiah? Whose family will he come from?"

They answered, "He will be a son of King David."*j*

43Jesus replied, "How then could the Spirit have David call the Messiah his Lord? David said,

44'The Lord said to my Lord:
Sit at my right side*k*
until I make your enemies
into a footstool for you.'

45If David called the Messiah his Lord, how can the Messiah be a son of King David?" 46No one was able to give Jesus an answer, and from that day on no one dared ask him any more questions.

Jesus Condemns the Pharisees and the Teachers of the Law of Moses
(Mark 12.38–40; Luke 11.37–52; 20.45–47)

23 Jesus said to the crowds and to his disciples:

2The Pharisees and the teachers of the Law are experts in the Law of Moses. 3So obey everything they teach you, but don't do as they do. After all, they say one thing and do something else.

4They pile heavy burdens on people's shoulders and won't lift a finger to help them. 5Everything they do is just to show off in front of others. They even make a big show of wearing Scripture verses on their fore-heads and arms, and they wear big tassels*l* for everyone to see. 6They love the best seats at banquets and the front seats in the meeting places. 7And when they are in the market, they like to have people greet them as their teachers.

8But none of you should be called a teacher. You have only one teacher, and all of you are like brothers and sisters. 9Don't call anyone on earth your father. All of you have the same Father in heaven. 10None of you should be called the leader. The Messiah is your only leader. 11Whoever is the greatest should be the servant of the others. 12If you put yourself above others, you will be put down. But if you humble yourself, you will be honored.

13-14 You Pharisees and teachers of the Law of Moses are in for trouble! You're nothing but showoffs. You lock people out of the kingdom of heaven. You won't go in yourselves, and you keep others from going in.*m*

15You Pharisees and teachers of the Law of Moses are in for trouble! You're nothing but showoffs. You travel over land and sea to win one follower. And when you have done so, you make that person twice as fit for hell as you are.

---

json of King David: See the note at 9.27.   *kright side*: The place of power and honor.   *lwearing Scripture verses on their foreheads and arms . . . tassels*: As a sign of their love for the Lord and his teachings, the Jewish people had started wearing Scripture verses in small leather boxes. But the Pharisees tried to show off by making the boxes bigger than necessary. The Jewish people were also taught to wear tassels on the four corners of their robes to show their love for God.   *mfrom going in*: Some manuscripts add, "You Pharisees and teachers are in for trouble! And you're nothing but showoffs! You cheat widows out of their homes and then pray long prayers just to show off. So you will be punished most of all."

16You are in for trouble! You are supposed to lead others, but you are blind. You teach that it doesn't matter if a person swears by the temple. But you say that it does matter if someone swears by the gold in the temple. 17You blind fools! Which is greater, the gold or the temple that makes the gold sacred?

18You also teach that it doesn't matter if a person swears by the altar. But you say that it does matter if someone swears by the gift on the altar. 19Are you blind? Which is more important, the gift or the altar that makes the gift sacred? 20Anyone who swears by the altar also swears by everything on it. 21And anyone who swears by the temple also swears by God, who lives there. 22To swear by heaven is the same as swearing by God's throne and by the one who sits on that throne.

23You Pharisees and teachers are showoffs, and you're in for trouble! You give God a tenth of the spices from your garden, such as mint, dill, and cumin. Yet you neglect the more important matters of the Law, such as justice, mercy, and faithfulness. These are the important things you should have done, though you should not have left the others undone either. 24You blind leaders! You strain out a small fly but swallow a camel.

25You Pharisees and teachers are showoffs, and you're in for trouble! You wash the outside of your cups and dishes, while inside there is nothing but greed and selfishness. 26You blind Pharisee! First clean the inside of a cup, and then the outside will also be clean.

27You Pharisees and teachers are in for trouble! You're nothing but showoffs. You're like tombs that have been whitewashed.[n] On the outside they are beautiful, but inside they are full of bones and filth. 28That's what you are like. Outside you look good, but inside you are evil and only pretend to be good.

29You Pharisees and teachers are nothing but showoffs, and you're in for trouble! You build monuments for the prophets and decorate the tombs of good people. 30And you claim that you would not have taken part with your ancestors in killing the prophets. 31But you prove that you really are the relatives of the ones who killed the prophets. 32So keep on doing everything they did. 33You are nothing but snakes and the children of snakes! How can you escape going to hell?

34I will send prophets and wise people and experts in the Law of Moses to you. But you will kill them or nail them to a cross or beat them in your meeting places or chase them from town to town. 35That's why you will be held guilty for the murder of every good person, beginning with the good man Abel. This also

[n]whitewashed: Tombs were whitewashed to keep anyone from accidentally touching them. A person who touched a dead body or a tomb was considered unclean and could not worship with the rest of the Jewish people.

includes Barachiah's son Zechariah,[o] the man you murdered between the temple and the altar. 36I can promise that you people living today will be punished for all these things!

Jesus Loves Jerusalem
(Luke 13.34, 35)

37Jerusalem, Jerusalem! Your people have killed the prophets and have stoned the messengers who were sent to you. I have often wanted to gather your people, as a hen gathers her chicks under her wings. But you wouldn't let me. 38And now your temple will be deserted. 39You will not see me again until you say,

"Blessed is the one who comes
in the name of the Lord."

The Temple Will Be Destroyed
(Mark 13.1, 2; Luke 21.5, 6)

24 After Jesus left the temple, his disciples came over and said, "Look at all these buildings!"

2Jesus replied, "Do you see these buildings? They will certainly all be torn down! Not one stone will be left in place."

Warning about Trouble
(Mark 13.3–13; Luke 21.7–19)

3Later, as Jesus was sitting on the Mount of Olives, his disciples came to him in private and asked, "When will this happen? What will be the sign of your coming and of the end of the world?"

4Jesus answered:

Don't let anyone fool you. 5Many will come and claim to be me. They will say that they are the Messiah, and they will fool many people.

6You will soon hear about wars and threats of wars, but don't be afraid. These things will have to happen first, but that is not the end. 7Nations and kingdoms will go to war against each other. People will starve to death, and in some places there will be earthquakes. 8But this is just the beginning of troubles.

9You will be arrested, punished, and even killed. Because of me, you will be hated by people of all nations. 10Many will give up and will betray and hate each other. 11Many false prophets will come and fool a lot of people. 12Evil will spread and cause many people to stop loving others. 13But if you keep on being faithful right to the end, you will be saved. 14When the good news about the kingdom has been preached all over the world and told to all nations, the end will come.

The Horrible Thing
(Mark 13.14–23; Luke 21.20–24)

15Someday you will see that "Horrible Thing" in the holy place, just as the prophet Daniel said. Everyone who reads this must try to understand! 16If you are living in Judea at that time, run to the mountains. 17If you are

---

[o]*Zechariah*: Genesis is the first book in the Jewish Scriptures, and it tells that Abel was the first person to be murdered. Second Chronicles is the last book in the Jewish Scriptures, and the last murder that it tells about is that of Zechariah.

on the roof[p] of your house, don't go inside to get anything. 18If you are out in the field, don't go back for your coat. 19It will be a terrible time for women who are expecting babies or nursing young children. 20And pray that you won't have to escape in winter or on a Sabbath.[q] 21This will be the worst time of suffering since the beginning of the world, and nothing this terrible will ever happen again. 22If God doesn't make the time shorter, no one will be left alive. But because of God's chosen ones, he will make the time shorter.

23Someone may say, "Here is the Messiah!" or "There he is!" But don't believe it. 24False messiahs and false prophets will come and work great miracles and signs. They will even try to fool God's chosen ones. 25But I have warned you ahead of time. 26If you are told that the Messiah is out in the desert, don't go there! And if you are told that he is in some secret place, don't believe it! 27The coming of the Son of Man will be like lightning that can be seen from east to west. 28Where there is a corpse, there will always be buzzards.[r]

When the Son of Man Appears
(Mark 13.24–27; Luke 21.25–28)

29Right after those days of suffering,

"The sun will become dark,
and the moon
will no longer shine.
The stars will fall,
and the powers in the sky[s]
will be shaken."

30Then a sign will appear in the sky. And there will be the Son of Man.[t] All nations on earth will weep when they see the Son of Man coming on the clouds of heaven with power and great glory. 31At the sound of a loud trumpet he will send his angels to bring his chosen ones together from all over the earth.

A Lesson from a Fig Tree
(Mark 13.28–31; Luke 21.29–33)

32Learn a lesson from a fig tree. When its branches sprout and start putting out leaves, you know that summer is near. 33So when you see all these things happening, you will know that the time has almost come.[u] 34I can promise you that some of the people living today will still be alive when all this happens.

[p]*roof*: In Palestine the houses usually had a flat roof. Stairs on the outside led up to the roof, which was made of beams and boards covered with packed earth. [q]*in winter or on a Sabbath*: In Palestine the winters are cold and rainy and make travel difficult. The Jewish people were not allowed to travel much more than half a mile on the Sabbath. For these reasons it was hard for them to escape from their enemies in the winter or on a Sabbath. [r]*Where there is a corpse, there will always be buzzards*: This saying may mean that when anything important happens, people soon know about it. Or the saying may mean that whenever something bad happens, curious people gather around and stare. But the word translated "buzzard" also means "eagle" and may refer to the Roman army, which had an eagle as its symbol. [s]*the powers in the sky*: In ancient times people thought that the stars were spiritual powers. [t]*And there will be the Son of Man*: Or "And it will be the Son of Man." [u]*the time has almost come*: Or "he (that is, the Son of Man) will soon be here."

35The sky and the earth won't last forever, but my words will.

No One Knows the Day or Time
(Mark 13.32–37; Luke 17.26–30, 34–36)

36No one knows the day or hour. The angels in heaven don't know, and the Son himself doesn't know.*v* Only the Father knows. 37When the Son of Man appears, things will be just as they were when Noah lived. 38People were eating, drinking, and getting married right up to the day that the flood came and Noah went into the big boat. 39They didn't know anything was happening until the flood came and swept them all away. That is how it will be when the Son of Man appears.

40Two men will be in the same field, but only one will be taken. The other will be left. 41Two women will be together grinding grain, but only one will be taken. The other will be left. 42So be on your guard! You don't know when your Lord will come. 43Homeowners never know when a thief is coming, and they are always on guard to keep one from breaking in. 44Always be ready! You don't know when the Son of Man will come.

Faithful and Unfaithful Servants
(Luke 12.35–48)

45Who are faithful and wise servants? Who are the ones the master will put in charge of giving the other servants their food supplies at the proper time? 46Servants are fortunate if their master comes and finds them doing their job. 47You may be sure that a servant who is always faithful will be put in charge of everything the master owns. 48But suppose one of the servants thinks that the master will not return until late. 49Suppose that evil servant starts beating all the other servants and eats and drinks with people who are drunk. 50If that happens, the master will surely come on a day and at a time when the servant least expects him. 51That servant will then be punished and thrown out with the ones who only pretended to serve their master. There they will cry and grit their teeth in pain.

A Story about Ten Girls

25 The kingdom of heaven is like what happened one night when ten girls took their oil lamps and went to a wedding to meet the groom.*w* 2Five of the girls were foolish and five were wise. 3The foolish ones took their lamps, but no extra oil. 4The ones who were wise took along extra oil for their lamps.

5The groom was late arriving, and the girls became drowsy and fell asleep. 6Then in the middle of the night someone shouted,

---

vand the Son himself doesn't know: These words are not in some manuscripts. *wto meet the groom*: Some manuscripts add "and the bride." It was the custom for the groom to go to the home of the bride's parents to get his bride. Young girls and other guests would then go with them to the home of the groom's parents, where the wedding feast would take place.

"Here's the groom! Come to meet him!"

7When the girls got up and started getting their lamps ready, 8the foolish ones said to the others, "Let us have some of your oil! Our lamps are going out."

9The girls who were wise answered, "There's not enough oil for all of us! Go and buy some for yourselves."

10While the foolish girls were on their way to get some oil, the groom arrived. The girls who were ready went into the wedding, and the doors were closed. 11Later the other girls returned and shouted, "Sir, sir! Open the door for us!"

12But the groom replied, "I don't even know you!"

13So, my disciples, always be ready! You don't know the day or the time when all this will happen.

A Story about Three Servants
(Luke 19.11–27)

14The kingdom is also like what happened when a man went away and put his three servants in charge of all he owned. 15The man knew what each servant could do. So he handed five thousand coins to the first servant, two thousand to the second, and one thousand to the third. Then he left the country.

16As soon as the man had gone, the servant with the five thousand coins used them to earn five thousand more. 17The servant who had two thousand coins did the same with his money and earned two thousand more. 18But the servant with one thousand coins dug a hole and hid his master's money in the ground.

19Some time later the master of those servants returned. He called them in and asked what they had done with his money. 20The servant who had been given five thousand coins brought them in with the five thousand that he had earned. He said, "Sir, you gave me five thousand coins, and I have earned five thousand more."

21"Wonderful!" his master replied. "You are a good and faithful servant. I left you in charge of only a little, but now I will put you in charge of much more. Come and share in my happiness!"

22Next, the servant who had been given two thousand coins came in and said, "Sir, you gave me two thousand coins, and I have earned two thousand more."

23"Wonderful!" his master replied. "You are a good and faithful servant. I left you in charge of only a little, but now I will put you in charge of much more. Come and share in my happiness!"

24The servant who had been given one thousand coins then came in and said, "Sir, I know that you are hard to get along with. You harvest what you don't plant and gather crops where you have not scattered seed. 25I was frightened and went out and hid your money in the ground. Here is every single coin!"

26The master of the servant told him, "You are lazy and good-for-nothing! You know that I harvest what I don't plant and gather crops where I have not scattered seed. 27You could have at least put my money in the bank, so that I could have earned interest on it."

28Then the master said, "Now your money will be taken away and given to the servant with ten thousand coins! 29Everyone who has something will be given more, and they will have more than enough. But everything will be taken from those who don't have anything. 30You are a worthless servant, and you will be thrown out into the dark where people will cry and grit their teeth in pain."

The Final Judgment

31When the Son of Man comes in his glory with all of his angels, he will sit on his royal throne. 32The people of all nations will be brought before him, and he will separate them, as shepherds separate their sheep from their goats.

33He will place the sheep on his right and the goats on his left. 34Then the king will say to those on his right, "My father has blessed you! Come and receive the kingdom that was prepared for you before the world was created. 35When I was hungry, you gave me something to eat, and when I was thirsty, you gave me something to drink. When I was a stranger, you welcomed me, 36and when I was naked, you gave me clothes to wear. When I was sick, you took care of me, and when I was in jail, you visited me."

37Then the ones who pleased the Lord will ask, "When did we give you something to eat or drink? 38When did we welcome you as a stranger or give you clothes to wear 39or visit you while you were sick or in jail?"

40The king will answer, "Whenever you did it for any of my people, no matter how unimportant they seemed, you did it for me."

41Then the king will say to those on his left, "Get away from me! You are under God's curse. Go into the everlasting fire prepared for the devil and his angels! 42I was hungry, but you did not give me anything to eat, and I was thirsty, but you did not give me anything to drink. 43I was a stranger, but you did not welcome me, and I was naked, but you did not give me any clothes to wear. I was sick and in jail, but you did not take care of me."

44Then the people will ask, "Lord, when did we fail to help you when you were hungry or thirsty or a stranger or naked or sick or in jail?"

45The king will say to them, "Whenever you failed to help any of my people, no matter how unimportant they seemed, you failed to do it for me."

46Then Jesus said, "Those people will be punished forever. But the ones who pleased God will have eternal life."

The Plot to Kill Jesus
(Mark 14.1, 2; Luke 22.1, 2; John 11.45–53)

26 When Jesus had finished teaching, he told his disci-

ples, 2"You know that two days from now will be Passover. That is when the Son of Man will be handed over to his enemies and nailed to a cross."

3At that time the chief priests and the nation's leaders were meeting at the home of Caiaphas the high priest. 4They planned how they could sneak around and have Jesus arrested and put to death. 5But they said, "We must not do it during Passover, because the people will riot."

At Bethany
(Mark 14.3–9; John 12.1–8)

6Jesus was in the town of Bethany, eating at the home of Simon, who had leprosy.[x] 7A woman came in with a bottle of expensive perfume and poured it on Jesus' head. 8But when his disciples saw this, they became angry. They said, "Why such a waste? 9We could have sold this perfume for a lot of money and given it to the poor."

10Jesus knew what they were thinking, and he said:

Why are you bothering this woman? She has done a beautiful thing for me. 11You will always have the poor with you, but you will not always have me. 12She has poured perfume on my body to prepare it for burial.[y] 13You may be sure that wherever the good news is told all over the world, people will remember what she has done. And they will tell others.

Judas and the Chief Priests
(Mark 14.10, 11; Luke 22.3–6)

14Judas Iscariot[z] was one of the twelve disciples. He went to the chief priests 15and asked, "How much will you give me if I help you arrest Jesus?" They paid Judas thirty silver coins, 16and from then on he started looking for a good chance to betray Jesus.

Jesus Eats the Passover Meal
with His Disciples
(Mark 14.12–21; Luke 22.7–13;
John 13.21–30)

17On the first day of the Feast of Thin Bread, Jesus' disciples came to him and asked, "Where do you want us to prepare the Passover meal?"

18Jesus told them to go to a certain man in the city and tell him, "Our teacher says, 'My time has come! I want to eat the Passover meal with my disciples in your home.'" 19They did as Jesus told them and prepared the meal.

20-21When Jesus was eating with his twelve disciples that evening, he said, "One of you will surely hand me over to my enemies."

22The disciples were very sad, and each one said to Jesus, "Surely, Lord, you don't mean me!"

23He answered, "One of you men who has eaten with me from this dish will betray me. 24The Son of Man will die, as the Scriptures say. But it's going to be terrible for the one who betrays me! That man would be better off if he had never been born."

25Judas said, "Teacher, surely you don't mean me!"

---

[x]leprosy: See the note at 8.2. [y]poured perfume on my body to prepare it for burial: The Jewish people taught that giving someone a proper burial was even more important than helping the poor. [z]Iscariot: See the note at 10.4.

"That's what you say!" Jesus replied. But later, Judas did betray him.

The Lord's Supper
(Mark 14.22–26; Luke 22.14–23;
1 Corinthians 11.23–25)

26During the meal Jesus took some bread in his hands. He blessed the bread and broke it. Then he gave it to his disciples and said, "Take this and eat it. This is my body."

27Jesus picked up a cup of wine and gave thanks to God. He then gave it to his disciples and said, "Take this and drink it. 28This is my blood, and with it God makes his agreement with you. It will be poured out, so that many people will have their sins forgiven. 29From now on I am not going to drink any wine, until I drink new wine with you in my Father's kingdom." 30Then they sang a hymn and went out to the Mount of Olives.

Peter's Promise
(Mark 14.27–31; Luke 22.31–34;
John 13.36–38)

31Jesus said to his disciples, "During this very night, all of you will reject me, as the Scriptures say,

'I will strike down
the shepherd,
and the sheep
will be scattered.'
32But after I am raised to life, I will go to Galilee ahead of you."

33Peter spoke up, "Even if all the others reject you, I never will!"

34Jesus replied, "I promise you that before a rooster crows tonight, you will say three times that you don't know me." 35But Peter said, "Even if I have to die with you, I will never say I don't know you."

All the others said the same thing.

Jesus Prays
(Mark 14.32–42; Luke 22.39–46)

36Jesus went with his disciples to a place called Gethsemane. When they got there, he told them, "Sit here while I go over there and pray."

37Jesus took along Peter and the two brothers, James and John.*[a]* He was very sad and troubled, 38and he said to them, "I am so sad that I feel as if I am dying. Stay here and keep awake with me."

39Jesus walked on a little way. Then he kneeled with his face to the ground and prayed, "My Father, if it is possible, don't make me suffer by having me drink from this cup.*[b]* But do what you want, and not what I want."

40He came back and found his disciples sleeping. So he said to Peter, "Can't any of you stay awake with me for just one hour? 41Stay awake and pray that you will not be tested. You want to do what is right, but you are weak."

42Again Jesus went to pray and said, "My Father, if there is no other way, and I must suffer, I will still do what you want."

43Jesus came back and found them sleeping again. They simply could not keep their eyes open. 44He left them and prayed the same prayer once more.

45Finally, Jesus returned to his

---

[a]the two brothers, James and John: The Greek text has "the two sons of Zebedee." See 27.56.
[b]having me drink from this cup: In the Scriptures "to drink from a cup" sometimes means to suffer. See the note at 20.22.

disciples and said, "Are you still sleeping and resting?*ᶜ* The time has come for the Son of Man to be handed over to sinners. **46**Get up! Let's go. The one who will betray me is already here."

Jesus Is Arrested
(Mark 14.43–50; Luke 22.47–53; John 18.3–12)

47Jesus was still speaking, when Judas the betrayer came up. He was one of the twelve disciples, and a large mob armed with swords and clubs was with him. They had been sent by the chief priests and the nation's leaders. **48**Judas had told them ahead of time, "Arrest the man I greet with a kiss."*ᵈ* **49**Judas walked right up to Jesus and said, "Hello, teacher." Then Judas kissed him.

50Jesus replied, "My friend, why are you here?"*ᵉ*

The men grabbed Jesus and arrested him. **51**One of Jesus' followers pulled out a sword. He struck the servant of the high priest and cut off his ear.

52But Jesus told him, "Put your sword away. Anyone who lives by fighting will die by fighting. **53**Don't you know that I could ask my Father, and right away he would send me more than twelve armies of angels? **54**But then, how could the words of the Scriptures come true, which say that this must happen?"

55Jesus said to the mob, "Why do you come with swords and clubs to arrest me like a criminal? Day after day I sat and taught in the temple, and you didn't arrest me. **56**But all this happened, so that what the prophets wrote would come true."

All of Jesus' disciples left him and ran away.

Jesus Is Questioned by the Jewish Council
(Mark 14.53–65; Luke 22.54, 55, 63–71; John 18.13, 14, 19–24)

57After Jesus had been arrested, he was led off to the house of Caiaphas the high priest. The nation's leaders and the teachers of the Law of Moses were meeting there. **58**But Peter followed along at a distance and came to the courtyard of the high priest's palace. He went in and sat down with the guards to see what was going to happen.

59The chief priests and the whole council wanted to put Jesus to death. So they tried to find some people who would tell lies about him in court.*ᶠ* **60**But they could not find any, even though many did come and tell lies. At last two men came forward **61**and said, "This man claimed that he would tear down God's temple and build it again in three days."

62The high priest stood up and asked Jesus, "Why don't you say something in your own defense? Don't you hear the charges they are making against you?" **63**But Jesus did not answer. So the high priest said, "With the living God looking on, you must tell the truth. Tell us, are you the Messiah, the Son of God?"*ᵍ*

ᶜAre you still sleeping and resting?: Or "You may as well keep on sleeping and resting." *ᵈthe man I greet with a kiss*: It was the custom for people to greet each other with a kiss on the cheek. *ᵉwhy are you here?*: Or "do what you came for." *ᶠsome people who would tell lies about him in court*: The Law of Moses taught that two witnesses were necessary before a person could be put to death. See verse 60. *ᵍSon of God*: One of the titles used for the kings of Israel.

64"That is what you say!" Jesus answered. "But I tell all of you,

'Soon you will see
the Son of Man
sitting at the right side[h]
of God All-Powerful
and coming on the clouds
of heaven.' "

65The high priest then tore his robe and said, "This man claims to be God! We don't need any more witnesses! You have heard what he said. 66What do you think?"

They answered, "He is guilty and deserves to die!" 67Then they spit in his face and hit him with their fists. Others slapped him 68and said, "You think you are the Messiah! So tell us who hit you!"

Peter Says He Does Not Know Jesus
(Mark 14.66–72; Luke 22.56–62; John 18.15–18, 25–27)

69While Peter was sitting out in the courtyard, a servant girl came up to him and said, "You were with Jesus from Galilee."

70But in front of everyone Peter said, "That's not so! I don't know what you are talking about!"

71When Peter had gone out to the gate, another servant girl saw him and said to some people there, "This man was with Jesus from Nazareth."

72Again Peter denied it, and this time he swore, "I don't even know that man!"

73A little while later some people standing there walked over to Peter and said, "We know that you are one of them. We can tell it because you talk like someone from Galilee."

74Peter began to curse and swear, "I don't know that man!"

Right then a rooster crowed, 75and Peter remembered that Jesus had said, "Before a rooster crows, you will say three times that you don't know me." Then Peter went out and cried hard.

Jesus Is Taken to Pilate
(Mark 15.1; Luke 23.1, 2; John 18.28–32)

27 Early the next morning all the chief priests and the nation's leaders met and decided that Jesus should be put to death. 2They tied him up and led him away to Pilate the governor.

The Death of Judas
(Acts 1.18, 19)

3When Judas learned that Jesus had been sentenced to death, he was sorry for what he had done. He returned the thirty silver coins to the chief priests and leaders 4and said, "I have sinned by betraying a man who has never done anything wrong."

"So what? That's your problem," they replied. 5Judas threw the money into the temple and then went out and hanged himself.

6The chief priests picked up the money and said, "This money was paid to have a man killed. We can't put it in the temple treasury." 7Then they had a meeting and decided to buy a field that belonged to someone who made clay pots. They wanted to use it as a graveyard for foreigners. 8That is why people still call that place "Field of Blood." 9So the words of the prophet Jeremiah came true,

[h]*right side*: See the note at 22.44.

"They took
the thirty silver coins,
the price of a person
among the people of Israel.
10They paid it
for a potter's field,[i]
as the Lord
had commanded me."

Pilate Questions Jesus
(Mark 15.2–5; Luke 23.3–5; John 18.33–38)

11Jesus was brought before Pilate the governor, who asked him, "Are you the King of the Jews?"

"Those are your words!" Jesus answered. 12And when the chief priests and leaders brought their charges against him, he did not say a thing. 13Pilate asked him, "Don't you hear what crimes they say you have done?" 14But Jesus did not say anything, and the governor was greatly amazed.

The Death Sentence
(Mark 15.6–15; Luke 23.13–26;
John 18.39–19.16)

15During Passover the governor always freed a prisoner chosen by the people. 16At that time a well-known terrorist named Jesus Barabbas[j] was in jail. 17So when the crowd came together, Pilate asked them, "Which prisoner do you want me to set free? Do you want Jesus Barabbas or Jesus who is called the Messiah?" 18Pilate knew that the leaders had brought Jesus to him because they were jealous.

19While Pilate was judging the case, his wife sent him a message. It said, "Don't have anything to do with that innocent man. I have had nightmares because of him."

20But the chief priests and the leaders convinced the crowds to ask for Barabbas to be set free and for Jesus to be killed. 21Pilate asked the crowd again, "Which of these two men do you want me to set free?"

"Barabbas!" they replied.

22Pilate asked them, "What am I to do with Jesus, who is called the Messiah?"

They all yelled, "Nail him to a cross!"

23Pilate answered, "But what crime has he done?"

"Nail him to a cross!" they yelled even louder.

24Pilate saw that there was nothing he could do and that the people were starting to riot. So he took some water and washed his hands[k] in front of them and said, "I won't have anything to do with killing this man. You are the ones doing it!"

25Everyone answered, "We and our descendants will take the blame for his death!"

26Pilate set Barabbas free. Then he ordered his soldiers to beat Jesus with a whip and nail him to a cross.

Soldiers Make Fun of Jesus
(Mark 15.16–21; John 19.2, 3)

27The governor's soldiers led Jesus into the fortress[l] and brought together

---

[i]*a potter's field*: Perhaps a field owned by someone who made clay pots. But it may have been a field where potters came to get clay or to make pots or to throw away their broken pieces of pottery. [j]*Jesus Barabbas*: Here and in verse 17 many manuscripts have "Barabbas." [k]*washed his hands*: To show that he was innocent. [l]*fortress*: The place where the Roman governor stayed. It was probably at Herod's palace west of Jerusalem, though it may have been Fortress Antonio north of the temple, where the Roman troops were stationed.

the rest of the troops. 28They stripped off Jesus' clothes and put a scarlet robe[m] on him. 29They made a crown out of thorn branches and placed it on his head, and they put a stick in his right hand. The soldiers kneeled down and pretended to worship him. They made fun of him and shouted, "Hey, you king of the Jews!" 30Then they spit on him. They took the stick from him and beat him on the head with it.

Jesus Is Nailed to a Cross
(Mark 15.22–32; Luke 23.27–43;
John 19.17–27)

31When the soldiers had finished making fun of Jesus, they took off the robe. They put his own clothes back on him and led him off to be nailed to a cross. 32On the way they met a man from Cyrene named Simon, and they forced him to carry Jesus' cross.

33They came to a place named Golgotha, which means "Place of the Skull."[m] 34There they gave Jesus some wine mixed with a drug to ease the pain. But when Jesus tasted what it was, he refused to drink it.

35The soldiers nailed Jesus to a cross and gambled to see who would get his clothes. 36Then they sat down to guard him. 37Above his head they put a sign that told why he was nailed there. It read, "This is Jesus, the King of the Jews." 38The soldiers also nailed two criminals on crosses, one to the right of Jesus and the other to his left.

39People who passed by said terrible things about Jesus. They shook their heads and 40shouted, "So you're the one who claimed you could tear down the temple and build it again in three days! If you are God's Son, save yourself and come down from the cross!"

41The chief priests, the leaders, and the teachers of the Law of Moses also made fun of Jesus. They said, 42"He saved others, but he can't save himself. If he is the king of Israel, he should come down from the cross! Then we will believe him. 43He trusted God, so let God save him, if he wants to. He even said he was God's Son." 44The two criminals also said cruel things to Jesus.

The Death of Jesus
(Mark 15.33–41; Luke 23.44–49;
John 19.28–30)

45At noon the sky turned dark and stayed that way until three o'clock. 46Then about that time Jesus shouted, "Eli, Eli, lema sabachthani?"[o] which means, "My God, my God, why have you deserted me?"

47Some of the people standing there heard Jesus and said, "He's calling for Elijah."[p] 48One of them at once ran and grabbed a sponge. He soaked it in wine, then put it on a stick and held it up to Jesus.

49Others said, "Wait! Let's see if Elijah will come[q] and save him."

---

[m]*scarlet robe*: This was probably a Roman soldier's robe. [n]*Place of the Skull*: The place was probably given this name because it was near a large rock in the shape of a human skull. [o]*Eli . . . sabachthani*: These words are in Aramaic, a language spoken in Palestine during the time of Jesus. [p]*Elijah*: In Aramaic the name "Elijah" sounds like "Eli," which means "my God." [q]*Elijah will come*: Many of the Jewish people expected the prophet Elijah to come and prepare the way for the Messiah.

50Once again Jesus shouted, and then he died.

51At once the curtain in the temple[r] was torn in two from top to bottom. The earth shook, and rocks split apart. 52Graves opened, and many of God's people were raised to life. 53Then after Jesus had risen to life, they came out of their graves and went into the holy city, where many people saw them.

54The officer and the soldiers guarding Jesus felt the earthquake and saw everything else that happened. They were frightened and said, "This man really was God's Son!"

55Many women were looking on from a distance. They had come with Jesus from Galilee to be of help to him. 56Mary Magdalene, Mary the mother of James and Joseph, and the mother of James and John[s] were some of these women.

Jesus Is Buried
(Mark 15.42–47; Luke 23.50–56; John 19.38–42)

57That evening a rich disciple named Joseph from the town of Arimathea 58went and asked for Jesus' body. Pilate gave orders for it to be given to Joseph, 59who took the body and wrapped it in a clean linen cloth. 60Then Joseph put the body in his own tomb that had been cut into solid rock[t] and had never been used. He rolled a big stone against the entrance to the tomb and went away.

61All this time Mary Magdalene and the other Mary were sitting across from the tomb.

62On the next day, which was a Sabbath, the chief priests and the Pharisees went together to Pilate. 63They said, "Sir, we remember what that liar said while he was still alive. He claimed that in three days he would come back from death. 64So please order the tomb to be carefully guarded for three days. If you don't, his disciples may come and steal his body. They will tell the people that he has been raised to life, and this last lie will be worse than the first one."[u]

65Pilate said to them, "All right, take some of your soldiers and guard the tomb as well as you know how." 66So they sealed it tight and placed soldiers there to guard it.

Jesus Is Alive
(Mark 16.1–8; Luke 24.1–12; John 20.1–10)

28 The Sabbath was over, and it was almost daybreak on Sunday when Mary Magdalene and the other Mary went to see the tomb. 2Suddenly a strong earthquake struck, and the Lord's angel came down from heaven. He rolled away the stone and sat on it. 3The angel looked as bright as lightning, and his clothes were white as snow. 4The guards shook from fear and fell down, as though they were dead.

5The angel said to the women, "Don't be afraid! I know you are looking for Jesus, who was nailed to a cross.

---

[r]curtain in the temple: There were two curtains in the temple. One was at the entrance, and the other separated the holy place from the most holy place that the Jewish people thought of as God's home on earth. The second curtain is probably the one that is meant. [s]of James and John: The Greek text has "of Zebedee's sons." See 26.37. [t]tomb . . . solid rock: Some of the Jewish people buried their dead in rooms carved into solid rock. A heavy stone was rolled against the entrance. [u]the first one: Probably the belief that Jesus is the Messiah.

6He is not here! God has raised him to life, just as Jesus said he would. Come, see the place where his body was lying. 7Now hurry! Tell his disciples that he has been raised to life and is on his way to Galilee. Go there, and you will see him. That is what I came to tell you."

8The women were frightened and yet very happy, as they hurried from the tomb and ran to tell his disciples. 9Suddenly Jesus met them and greeted them. They went near to him, held on to his feet, and worshiped him. 10Jesus said to them, "Don't be afraid! Tell my followers to go to Galilee. They will see me there."

Report of the Guard

11While the women were on their way, some soldiers who had been guarding the tomb went into the city. They told the chief priests everything that had happened. 12So the chief priests met with the leaders and decided to bribe the soldiers with a lot of money. 13They said to the soldiers, "Tell everyone that Jesus' disciples came during the night and stole his body while you were asleep. 14If the governor[v] hears about this, we will talk to him. You won't have anything to worry about." 15The soldiers took the money and did what they were told. The Jewish people still tell each other this story.

What Jesus' Followers Must Do
(Mark 16.14–18; Luke 24.36–49; John 20.19–23; Acts 1.6–8)

16Jesus' eleven disciples went to a mountain in Galilee, where Jesus had told them to meet him. 17They saw him and worshiped him, but some of them doubted.

18Jesus came to them and said:

I have been given all authority in heaven and on earth! 19Go to the people of all nations and make them my disciples. Baptize them in the name of the Father, the Son, and the Holy Spirit, 20and teach them to do everything I have told you. I will be with you always, even until the end of the world.

[v]*governor*: Pontius Pilate.

Word List

Aaron The brother of Moses. Only he and his descendants were to serve as priests and offer sacrifices for the people of Israel.

Abel The second son of Adam and Eve and the younger brother of Cain, who killed him, after God accepted Abel's offering and refused Cain's.

Abijah A descendant of Aaron. King David divided the priests into twenty-four groups, and Abijah was head of the eighth group.

Abimelech The Philistine king of Gath when David escaped from there by pretending to be crazy. See the title of Psalm 34. He is called Achish in 1 Samuel 21.10—22.1.

Abraham The first great ancestor of the people of Israel. He was the husband of Sarah and the father of Isaac. Abraham put his faith in God, and God promised to bless everyone on earth because of Abraham.

Adam The first man and the husband of Eve.

Agrippa (1) Herod Agrippa was king of Judea A.D. 41–44 and mistreated Christians (Acts 12.1–5). (2) Agrippa II was the son of Herod Agrippa and ruled Judea A.D. 44–53. He and his sister Bernice listened to Paul defend himself (Acts 25.13–26, 32).

Agur, Son of Jakeh A wise man, otherwise unknown. Agur wrote some of the proverbs. See Proberbs 30.1.

Ahimelech A priest at Nob who gave food and a sword to David when he fled from Saul. See the title of Psalm 52.

aloes A sweet-smelling spice that was mixed with myrrh and used as a perfume.

altar A raised structure where sacrifices and offerings were presented to God or gods. Altars could be made of rocks, packed earth, metal or pottery.

amen A Hebrew word used after a prayer or a blessing and meaning, "Let it be that way."

ancestor Someone born one or more generations earlier in a family line, such as a grandparent or great-grandparent.

angel A supernatural being who tells God's messages or protects God's people.

Antipas The father of Herod the Great and ruler of Judea 55–43 B.C. He was also known as Antipater.

apostle A person chosen by Christ to take his message to others.

Aram-naharaim A territory in northern Mesopotamia. The name means Arameans from the land of the Two Rivers. See the title of Psalm 60.

Aram-zobah An Aramean kingdom north of Damascus. See the title of Psalm 60 and 2 Samuel 8.3–13.

Aramaic A language closely related to Hebrew. It was spoken by many Jews including Jesus during New Testament times.

Asaph One of David's musicians. He wrote many psalms and also sang at the dedication of Solomon's temple. See the titles of Psalms 50 and 73–83.

Asia A Roman province in what is today modern Turkey.

Augustus This is the title meaning "honored" that the Romans gave to Octavian when he began ruling the Roman world in 27 B.C. He was Emperor when Jesus was born (Luke 2.1).

Babylon A large city in south-central Mesopotamia, the capital of the kingdom of Babylonia. The Babylonians defeated the southern kingdom of Judah in the sixth century B.C. and forced many of its people to live in Babylonia.

barley A grain something like wheat and used to make bread.

Bashan Flatlands and wooded hills in southern Syria, northeast of Lake Galilee. It was known for its fat cattle and fine grain. See Psalm 68.15, 16.

Benjamin One of the tribes of Israel. It occupied land between Bethel and Jerusalem. The people of this tribe descended from Benjamin, the younger of Jacob and

Rachel's two sons. When the ten northern tribes of Israel broke away following the death of Solomon, only the tribes of Benjamin and Judah were left to form the southern kingdom.

Cain The first son of Adam and Eve and the brother of Abel.

Christ A Greek word meaning "the Chosen One" and used to translate the Hebrew word "Messiah." It is used in the New Testament both as a title and a name for Jesus.

circumcise To cut off the foreskin from the male organ. This is done for Jewish boys as part of a religious ceremony eight days after they are born to show that they belong to God's people. God's command to Abraham (Genesis 17.9–14) was to circumcise all males on the eighth day. Jesus' circumcision on the eighth day is reported in Luke 2.21.

citizen A person who is given special rights and privileges by a nation or state. In return, a citizen was expected to be loyal to that nation or state.

commandments God's rules for his people to live by.

council A leading group of Jewish men who were allowed by the Roman government to meet and make certain decisions for their people.

cumin A plant with small seeds used for seasoning food.

David The most famous ancestor of the Jewish people and the most powerful king Israel ever had. They hoped that one of his descendants would always be their king.

Day of Atonement The one day each year (the tenth day after the Jewish new year's day in the fall) when the high priest went into the most holy part of the temple and sprinkled some of the blood of a sacrificed bull on the sacred chest. This was done so that the people's sins would be forgiven. This holy day is called Yom Kippur in Hebrew.

demons and *evil spirits* Supernatural beings that do harmful things to people and sometimes cause them to do bad things. In the New Testament they are sometimes called "unclean spirits," because people under their power were thought to be unclean and unfit to worship God.

descendant Someone born one or more generations later in a family line, such as a grandchild or great-grandchild.

devil The chief of the demons and evil spirits, also known as "Satan."

disciple Someone who was a follower of Jesus and learned from him.

Doeg of Edom An Edomite who worked for King Saul as the head of his shepherds. He was known to be ruthless and conniving. See the title of Psalm 52 and 1 Samuel 21–22.

Edom A kingdom south of the Dead Sea as far as the Gulf of Aqaba. The Edomites descended from Esau, the twin brother of Jacob.

Elijah A prophet who spoke for God in the ninth century B.C. Many Jews in later centuries thought Elijah would return to get things ready for the coming of the Lord.

elders Men whose age and wisdom made them respected leaders.

Emperor The ruler who lived in the city of Rome and governed all the land around the Mediterranean Sea.

Ephraim One of the most important tribes of northern Israel. It occupied the land north of Benjamin and south of Manasseh. The people of this tribe descended from Ephraim, Joseph's second son.

Epicureans People who followed the teachings of a man named Epicurus, who taught that happiness should be a person's main goal in life.

eternal life Life that is the gift of God and never ends.

Ethan the Ezrahite One of David's musicians. See the title of Psalm 89.

Ethiopia The extensive territory south of Egypt called Cush in Hebrew, traditionally translated as Ethiopia. In Bible times it included within its borders most of modern Sudan and present day Ethiopia.

evil spirits See "demons."

exile The time in Jewish history (597–539 B.C.) when the Babylonians took away most of the people of Jerusalem and Judah as prisoners of war and made them live in Babylonia.

Feast of Thin Bread The days after Passover when Jews eat a kind of thin, flat bread made without yeast to remember how God freed the people of Israel from slavery in Egypt and give them a fresh start.

Felix The Roman governor of Judea A.D. 52–60, who listened to Paul speak and kept him in jail.

Festival of Shelters This festival celebrates the period of forty years when the people of Israel walked through the desert and lived in small shelters. This happy celebration takes place each year in connection with the fall harvest season. Its name in Hebrew is Sukkoth.

Festus The Roman governor after Felix, who sent Paul to stand trial in Rome.

Gath One of the five major Philistine towns on the coastal plain of southern Palestine.

Generation One way of describing a group of people who live during the same period of time. The time of one generation is often understood to be about forty years. See Psalm 95.10.

Gentile Someone who is not a Jew.

Glory The magnificence of God's presence that inspires awe and worship.

God's kingdom God's rule over people, both in this life and in the next.

God's Law God's rules for his people to live by. They are found in the Old Testament, especially in the first five books.

God's Tent The tent where the people of Israel worshiped God before the temple was built.

Greek The language in which the New Testament was written.

Hagar A personal servant of Sarah, the wife of Abraham. When Sarah could not have any children, she followed the ancient custom of letting her husband have a child by Hagar, her servant woman. The boy's name was Ishmael.

Hebrew The language used by the people of Israel and for the writing of most of the Old Testament.

Heman the Ezrahite One of David's musicians. See the title of Psalm 88.

Hermes The Greek god of skillful speaking and the messenger of the other Greek gods.

Herod (1) Herod the Great was the king of all Palestine 37–4 B.C. He ruled Judea at the time Jesus was born. (2) Herod Antipas was the son of Herod the Great and the ruler of Galilee 4 B.C.–A.D. 39, during the time of John the Baptist and Jesus. (3) Herod Agrippa I, the grandson of Herod the Great, ruled Palestine A.D. 41–44.

Hezekiah King of Judah during the Assyrian attack on Jerusalem in 701 B.C., known for his loyalty to the LORD.

high priest See "priest."

Holy One A name for the Savior that God had promised to send. See "Savior."

hyssop A bush with bunches of small, white flowers. A bunch of hyssop was used for sprinkling blood and water in religious ceremonies. These ceremonies made people rightly prepared to worship God after having a bad skin disease. In a similar way, Psalm 51.7 mentions using hyssop in making a person rightly prepared to worship God by taking away sin.

incense A material that makes a sweet smell when burned and is used in the worship of God.

Isaac The second of the three great ancestors of the people of Israel. He was the son of Abraham and father of Jacob.

Isaiah A prophet from Jerusalem, who lived during the eighth century B.C. He served as a prophet during the rule of four different kings of Judah, between the years 740–700 B.C.

Israel See Jacob/Israel.

Jacob/Israel The third great ancestor of the people of Israel. He was the son of Isaac. His name was changed to Israel when he struggled with God at the Jabbok River.

Jeduthun One of David's musicians. See the titles of Psalms 39, 62, 77.

Joab The commander of David's army during most of his reign. See the title of Psalm 60.

Joseph The older son of Jacob and Rachel. He was the father of Ephraim and Manasseh, whose descendants formed two of the most important northern tribes.

Judah One of the tribes of Israel. It occupied the hill country between the Dead Sea and the coastal flatlands. The people of this tribe descended from Judah, the fourth son of Jacob and Leah. When the ten northern tribes of Israel broke away following the death of Solomon, only the tribes of Judah and Benjamin were left to form the southern kingdom.

judges Leaders chosen by the Lord for the people of Israel after the time of Joshua and before the time of the kings.

Kadesh A town in the desert of Paran southwest of the Dead Sea, also known as Kadesh-Barnea. It was near the southern border of Israel and the western border of Edom.

King Lemuel of Massa King of Massa, a country possibly located in northern Arabia. King Lemuel wrote a few of the proverbs. See Proverbs 31.1.

Korah A Levite family of the clan of Kohath whose people formed one of the major groups of temple singers. The Korahites were also known as temple gatekeepers (1 Chronicles 9.19) and temple bakers (1 Chronicles 9.31).

Law and the Prophets The sacred writings of the Jews in Jesus' day (the first two of the three sections of the Old Testament).

Law of Moses and *Law of the Lord* Usually refers to the first five books of the Old Testament, but sometimes to the entire Old Testament.

Leviathan A legendary sea monster representing revolt and evil, also known from Canaanite writings. Psalm 74.14 celebrates its defeat by God.

Levite A member of the tribe of Levi, from which priests were chosen. Men from this tribe who were not priests helped with the work in the temple.

Lᴏʀᴅ The word "Lᴏʀᴅ" in capital letters stands for the Hebrew consonants *YHWH,* the personal names of God. The word "Lord" represents the Hebrew term *Adonai,* the general word for "Lord." By late Old Testament times Jews considered God's personal name too holy to be pronounced. So they said *Adonai,* "Lord," whenever they read the Hebrew consonants *YHWH.* When the Jewish scribes first translated the Hebrew Scriptures into ancient Greek, they translated the personal name of God as *Kurios,* "Lord." Since then most translations, including the *Contemporary English Version,* have followed the Jewish example and avoided using the personal name of God.

Manasseh One of the most important tribes of northern Israel. It occupied two areas of land. One was east of the Jordan River, from the Jabbok River north to include all of Bashan. The other was on the west side of the Jordan River and went all the way to the Mediterranean Sea. Its northern boundary began a few miles south of Lake Galilee and went as far south as the border with Ephraim. The people of this tribe descended from Manasseh, Joseph's first son.

Messiah A Hebrew word meaning "the Chosen One." See "Christ."

mint A garden plant used for seasoning and medicine.

Moab A country east of the Dead Sea. Its people descended from Moab, the son of Lot, who was Abraham's nephew.

Moses The leader of the people of Israel when God rescued them from Egypt.

Mt. Hermon One of the highest mountains in the Near East, with an elevation of 9,230 feet. Located about 45 miles north of Lake Galilee, its three peaks tower over the upper Jordan River valley. In Hebrew the name means "sacred" or "forbidden."

Mt. Lebanon A mountain range that stretches about 100 miles north and south along the coast of Phoenicia. In Hebrew the name means "white," and it was known for its white peaks and cedar forests.

Mt. Mizar Probably a name for one of the lesser peaks of Mt. Hermon. Possibly a way of referring to the small size of Mt. Zion. In Hebrew the name means "small." See Psalm 42.6.

myrrh A valuable sweet-smelling powder used in perfume.

Naphtali One of the tribes of Israel. Its people descended from Naphtali, the second son of Jacob and Bilhah. The tribe occupied land north and west of Lake Galilee.

Nazarenes A name that was sometimes used for the followers of Jesus, who came from the small town of Nazareth.

Noah When God destroyed the world by a flood, Noah and his family were kept safe in a big boat that God had told him to build.

paradise The place where God's people go when they die, often understood as another name for heaven.

Passover A day each year in the spring when Jews celebrate the time God rescued them from slavery in Egypt.

Pentecost A Jewish festival fifty days

after Passover to celebrate the wheat harvest.

Pharisees A large group of Jews who thought they could best serve God by strictly obeying the laws of the Old Testament as well as their own teachings.

Philistia The fertile strip of land along the Mediterranean coast controlled by the Philistine people. This land began at the Brook of Egypt, below Gaza in the south, and ended at the town of Joppa in the north. Philistia was often at war with Israel.

Phoenicia The territory along the Mediterranean Sea controlled by the cities of Tyre, Sidon, Arvad and Byblos. The coast of modern Lebanon covers about the same area.

pit or *deep pit* The place of punishment for demons and evil spirits.

priest A man who led the worship in the temple and offered sacrifices. Some of the more important priests were called "chief priests," and the most important priest was called the "high priest."

Promised One A title for the Savior that God promised to send. See "Savior."

prophesy See "prophet."

Prophet A person who delivers a message from God to another person or to a group. Often a prophet's message tells what will happen in the future. To speak as a prophet is thus to "prophesy."

Proverb A wise saying that is short and easy to remember.

Psalm A Hebrew poem that could be used as a song or a prayer. Psalms could be prayed by individuals or sung by groups in worship of God. Some of the psalms thank and praise God. Others ask God to take away sins or to give protection, comfort, vengeance or mercy.

rue A garden plant used for seasoning and medicine.

Sabbath The seventh day of the week when Jews worship and do not work, in obedience to the commandment.

Sacrifice/Offering Gifts to God of certain animals, grains, fruits, and sweet-smelling spices. Israelites offered sacrifices to give thanks to God, to beg for forgiveness, to make a payment for a wrong, or to ask for God's blessing. Some sacrifices were completely burned on the altar. In other sacrifices, a portion was offered to the

LORD and the remaining portions were eaten by the priests or ordinary people.

Sadducees A small and powerful group of Jews who were closely connected with the high priests and who accepted only the first five books of the Old Testament as their Bible. They also did not believe in life after death.

Samaria A district between Judea and Galilee. The people of Samaria, called Samaritans, worshiped God differently from the Jews and did not get along with them.

Sarah The wife of Abraham and the mother of Isaac. When she was very old, God promised her that she would have a son.

Satan See "devil."

save To rescue people from the power of evil, to give them new life, and to place them under God's care. See "Savior."

Savior The one who rescues people from the power of evil, gives them new life, and places them under God's care. See "save."

Scriptures The sacred writings known as the Old Testament. These were first written in Hebrew and Aramaic, then translated into Greek about two centuries before the birth of Jesus. This Greek translation, known as the Septuagint, was used both by Jews and Christians in the first century.

Sin Turning away from God and disobeying the teachings of God.

Solomon One of King David's sons. After David's death, Solomon took his place as king and became widely known for his wisdom. He wrote many of the proverbs and two of the psalms. See Proverbs 10.1 and 25.1; Psalms 72 and 127.

Son of Man A name often used by Jesus to refer to himself. It is also found in the book of Daniel and refers to the one to whom God has given the power to rule.

Stoics Followers of a man named Zeno, who believed that nature was controlled by the gods and who taught that people should learn self-control.

taxes and *tax collectors* Special fees collected by rulers, usually part of the value of a citizen's crop, property, or income. There were also market taxes to be paid, and customs taxes were collected at ports and border crossings. The wealthy Zacchaeus (Luke 19.1–10) was a tax collector who collected taxes at a border crossing near Jericho. Jews hired by the Roman government to collect taxes from other Jews were hated by their own people.

temple   A building used as a place of worship. The Jewish temple was in Jerusalem.

Temple Festival   In 165 B.C. the Jewish people recaptured the Jerusalem temple from their enemies and made it fit for worship again. They celebrate this event in December of each year by a festival which they call "dedication" (Hanukkah). In the New Testament it is mentioned only in John 10.22.

Theophilus   The name means "someone God loves" and is found only in Luke 1.3 and Acts 1.1. Nothing else is known about him.

Way   In the book of Acts the Christian religion is sometimes called "the Way" or "the Way of the Lord" or "God's Way."

Wisdom   The cleverness, common sense, and practical skill needed to solve the everyday problems of life. Wisdom is sometimes pictured as a wise woman who invites people to use good judgment. In Proverbs 8, Wisdom is pictured as helping God plan and build the universe.

Zebulun   One of the tribes of Israel. It occupied land that was north of Manasseh and that stretched from the eastern end of Mt. Carmel to Mt. Tabor. The people of this tribe descended from Zebulun, the sixth son of Jacob and Leah.

Zeus   The chief god of the Greeks.

Zion   Another name for Jerusalem. It can also refer to the hill in Jerusalem where the temple was built.

Ziph   A town in the hill country of southern Judah where David hid while running away from King Saul. See the title of Psalm 54 and 1 Samuel 23.19; 26.1.

PALESTINE IN THE TIME OF JESUS

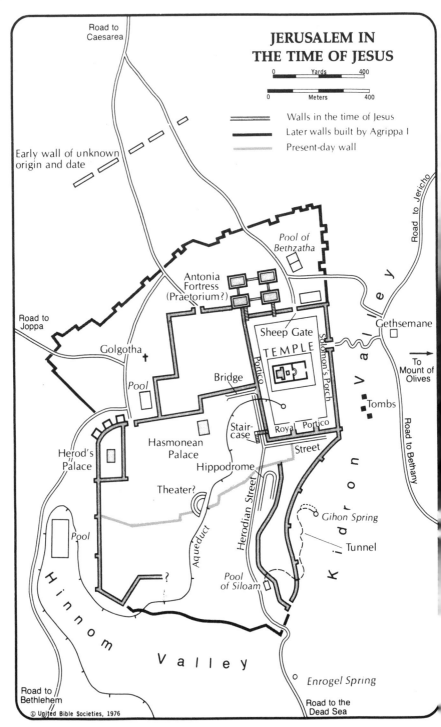

JERUSALEM IN THE TIME OF JESUS

Walls in the time of Jesus
Later walls built by Agrippa I
Present-day wall

Road to Caesarea

Early wall of unknown origin and date

Road to Joppa

Golgotha

Pool

Herod's Palace

Hasmonean Palace

Theater?

Pool

Aqueduct

Road to Bethlehem

© United Bible Societies, 1976

Antonia Fortress (Praetorium?)

Pool of Bethzatha

Sheep Gate

TEMPLE

Bridge

Staircase

Royal Portico

Street

Hippodrome

Herodian Street

Pool of Siloam

Gihon Spring

Tunnel

Enrogel Spring

Road to the Dead Sea

Gethsemane

To Mount of Olives

Tombs

Road to Jericho

Road to Bethany

Kidron Valley

Hinnom Valley

Solomon's Porch

Portico

viii